EDITORIAL RESEARCH REPORTS ON

THE
WOMEN'S
MOVEMENT

Published by Congressional Quarterly, Inc.
1414 22nd Street, N.W.
Washington, D.C. 20037

About the Cover

The cover art was designed and executed by Jack Barrett and Joe Tonelli.

Published in August 1973

Library of Congress Catalogue Card Number 73-84338
International Standard Book Number 0-87187-046-0

Editorial Research Reports
Editor Emeritus, Richard M. Boeckel
Editor, William B. Dickinson, Jr.
Managing Editor, Hoyt Gimlin
Production Supervisor, Richard C. Young
Art Director, Howard E. Chapman

CONTENTS

Foreword v

Women's Consciousness Raising 1

Marriage: Changing Institution 21

Status of Women 41

Child Care 65

Crime of Rape 85

Women Voters 105

Legalization of Prostitution 125

Coeducation: New Growth 145

Child Adoption 165

FOREWORD

A decade has passed since the bible of the new feminism, Betty Friedan's *Feminine Mystique*, began to stir the consciousness of American womanhood to the male dominance of the world in which they lived. In the intervening years, the organized militancy of "women's lib" publicized the cause and provoked a series of strong responses—for and against. Now after an era of bra-burning symbolism, the women's movement seems to have given way to a new phase that is far less dramatic but perhaps much farther reaching.

To Carl Degler, the author-historian: "The women's movement is the most radical social phenomenon in all history." A good case can be made for that assertion if the movement does indeed achieve its underlying goal of reconditioning the thinking of men and women to accept sex equality as the norm of social and personal and business behavior. Whether society is moving toward that golden sequel is subject to the interpretation of a great flow of statistical information and personal observation.

Nearly every recitation of fact must be followed with a "but" or "on the other hand." For instance, more women than ever before are in the labor force—many in jobs opened to them for the first time—but the gap between men's salaries and their own has widened rather than narrowed. Recent surveys indicate growing support for status-of-women issues espoused by the movement. But, the polls also tell us, the support is actually higher among men than among women. From such fragments of evidence, only the foolish find material for prophecy. Yet it can safely be said that the movement has refused to fade into oblivion and become merely a passing fad on the American scene.

Hoyt Gimlin
Managing Editor

August 1973
Washington, D.C.

Women's Consciousness Raising

by

Helen B. Shaffer

RESURGENCE OF FEMINISM IN NEW FORM
Emphasis of Feminism on Psychological Factor
Major Success of Raising Popular Awareness
Influence on News Media; Women's Magazines
Dual Phases and Aims of Sexual-Equality Drive

EVOLUTION OF U.S. WOMEN'S PROTEST
Convergence of Factors Conducive to Protest
Analyses of Woman's Role as the 'Second Sex'
Founding of Activist Groups to Attack Sex Bias
Persistence of the Movement Despite Divisions

CONSEQUENCES OF CONSCIOUSNESS RAISING
Shock Aspects of 'Women's Lib' Militancy
Small-Group Exchanges of Personal Testimony
Question of Reaching Beyond the Middle Class
Paying the Price for Full Equality of the Sexes

1 9 7 3
July 5

WOMEN'S CONSCIOUSNESS RAISING

T HE TIME for bra-burning may have passed but this is not to say that the women's liberation movement has played itself out. On the contrary, the currents of change released by the movement are still coursing through the nation and their effects are being registered in many areas of American life. The movement's crowning achievement is that it has raised the consciousness of the people on the issue of sexual equality. As a result, women are acting—and men are reacting—as never before to the ideas fostered by the movement.

Where it will all end no one can say, but the portents of major social change loom large. For the feminist revival that began in the latter half of the 1960s is heading toward a far more fundamental change than that sought by the suffragists of a half-century ago or even by the "equal rights" fighters of the more recent past. The underlying goal is no less than a reconditioning of the American people to accept sex equality as the norm of social and personal behavior. It would mean a reordering of the way men and women customarily feel about each other in every relationship of life: as father-daughter, mother-son, sister-brother, teacher-student, boy friend-girl friend, husband-wife, employer-employee, doctor-patient.

A feminist leader, Wilma Scott Heide, president of the National Organization of Women (Now), has described the women's liberation movement as "the most profound universal behavioral revolution the world has ever known."[1] Authors of a comprehensive study of the movement call it "as much a state of mind as it is a movement."[2] This is doubtless because the area of struggle is not merely economic, social and political, but psychological, intellectual, and emotional. The embattled women today are conducting a war for the minds and feelings of women primarily, men secondarily. Through liberating women from viewing themselves as the inferior sex, it

---

[1] Quoted in advertisement for a book on feminism in the magazine *Ms.*, July 1972, p. 23.
[2] Judith Hole and Ellen Levine, *Rebirth of Feminism* (1971).

is expected that men will be liberated from the burdens of dominance. When society no longer imposes "sex-role segregation" on its members, both sexes will gain and presumably will get along a lot better with each other.

All of this is still conjectural and controversial, of course. This latest phase of the feminist movement has had only a few years to make its case. It still speaks with many voices, some angry and strident, most in sharp disagreement with the others.[3] The intellectuals of the movement are still putting together the body of theory that will explain and justify their version of woman's historic role and their vision of a better future.

Emphasis of Feminism on Psychological Factor

A fundamental question has yet to be answered: Are the women of the liberation seeking a valid goal or are they pursuing a will-o'-the-wisp, a form of sexual equality that can never be achieved? Many who have spoken on the issue believe the liberationists are fighting against a natural order that decrees a more passive, nurturing role for females, complementing the more aggressive and venturesome male. Even those who sympathize with the crusade to remove sex discriminatory practices in education, employment and politics may still object to the liberationist view that, except in their reproductive functions, the differences between the sexes are inconsequential.

Many women do not accept the liberationists' version of womanhood as authentic and even within the movement there is much dissent and confusion. Some women confess that their pro-liberation thinking is at odds with their anti-liberation feelings;[4] they have been intellectually convinced but their hearts still belong to the old order. Midge Decter, a writer who might have served as the very model of the successful, liberated, intellectual woman, has repeatedly attacked the movement as an absurdity, the work of a few maladjusted women, and not due for a long life.[5] But opinions on women's liberation may depend on which aspect of the movement is taken as its essence. Discounting the extremists still leaves a

---

[3] A woman participating in Women United, a coalition to support the Equal Rights Amendment to the Constitution, said: "The absolutely only feminist issue we all agree on is the amendment and were conversation to stray from that subject for more than 30 seconds, the group might well disintegrate into a not-too-pleasant free-for-all."— quoted by Judith Hole and Ellen Levine, *Rebirth of Feminism* (1971).

[4] See Nora Ephron's columns in *Esquire*. Also see Kathleen M. Snow, "My Liberated Mind Has a Wuthering Heights Heart," *Harper's*, July 1973, p. 87.

[5] See Midge Decter, *The New Chastity and Other Arguments Against Women's Liberation* (1972), *The Liberated Woman and Other Essays* (1971), and "Toward the New Chastity," *The Atlantic*, August 1972, pp. 42-55.

solid core of complaint about women's status and the response to the movement would indicate that it is far more than a fad. Women who have long worked in conventional ways to reduce sex discrimination in the law, in education, and in employment recognize the achievement of the more flamboyant liberationists in raising the consciousness of the nation on the woman question.

Major Success of Raising Popular Awareness

Women have made many gains in the few years since "women's lib" became a popular byword for latter-day feminism. These range from approval by Congress of the 27th (Equal Rights) Amendment *(see box)* to successful promotion of the use of Ms. in place of Miss or Mrs. The Equal Rights Amendment was approved and sent to the states for ratification on March 22, 1972, after having been introduced in every Congress for 49 years. It awaits ratification by the required three-fourths (38) of the states.[6] Acceptance of Ms., put forth to equal the score with Mr. in not disclosing marital status, was doubtless encouraged by its convenience for business use when the marital status of a female addressee is unknown. Even a presidential agency, the President's Commission on White House Fellows, now uses Ms. in addressing mail to women.

Feminist lobbying and litigation have knocked down numerous other barriers to sexual equality, especially in the field of employment. The academic world, one of the strongest bastions of male supremacy, has begun to respond to feminist pressure. Growing female visibility in politics was evident at the 1972 presidential nominating conventions. Several strong new female figures have emerged on the national political

---

[6] As of mid-1973, the legislatures of 30 states had voted for ratification although one of the states, Nebraska, rescinded its vote. The other 29 were: Alaska, California, Colorado, Connecticut, Delaware, Hawaii, Idaho, Iowa, Kansas, Kentucky, Maryland, Michigan, Massachusetts, Minnesota, New Hampshire, New Jersey, New Mexico, New York, Oregon, Pennsylvania, Rhode Island, Tennessee, Texas, South Dakota, Vermont, Washington, West Virginia, Wisconsin and Wyoming. Ratification had been voted down in 13 states: Alabama, Arkansas, Florida, Illinois, Indiana, Maine, Missouri, Nevada, North Carolina, North Dakota, Oklahoma, South Carolina and Utah. Ratification may be voted until March 22, 1979, by any of the states regardless of prior rejection.

scene, among them Shirley Chisholm, the black congress-woman from Brooklyn. In 1972 congressional elections, women gained one seat in the House, for a total of 14,[7] but the only woman senator, Margaret Chase Smith (R Maine), was defeated. Among the state legislatures, the number of women members rose from 344 to 441.

The movement's most noteworthy success, however, is not measurable by the number of women appointed and elected to office or the number of lawsuits that have succeeded in overthrowing sex-discriminatory practices. Its greatest triumph has been that it has raised the consciousness of the nation on the entire question of the role of the female in American society. For women, consciousness raising has meant a sharpened realization of their personal stake in women's rights, a kind of personal sensitizing to the issue that leads to a feeling of group solidarity with other women and gives them courage to rebel against their life situation. For American men, consciousness raising has meant a realization, often discomforting, that sex equality is a live issue and that the women are serious about their efforts to realize it.

Until the women's protest dramatized feminist demands and sought to analyze the sources of feminine discontent, few American men evinced much interest in the subject. Feminism frankly bored them; they considered the issues trivial, raised by neurotics who had failed as "real women." Many men are still irritated by or contemptuous of the movement, but they can scarcely ignore it or be unaware that, for good or ill, it heralds changes that can affect the lives of all.

The movement has thus succeeded in carrying the cause of sex equality beyond the orbit of feminist circles to make it a major issue of the day. The Academy of Political and Social Science in 1971 picked it as one of "seven polarizing issues in America today...[that] appeared to be commanding the greatest public interest."[8] *The American Scholar's* autumn 1972 issue devoted 28 pages to a transcript of a discussion of the movement. Women's caucuses or similar groups have been formed

---

[7] Two additional women were elected to the House in 1973 to fill vacancies created by the deaths of their husbands. They are Mrs. Hale Boggs (D La.) and Mrs. George W. Collins (D Ill.). The 14 elected in November 1972 were: Reps. Bella S. Abzug (D N.Y.), Yvonne Brathwaite Burke (D Calif.), Shirley Chisholm (D N.Y.), Ella T. Grasso (D Conn.). Edith Green (D Ore.), Martha W. Griffiths (D Mich), Julia Butler Hansen (D Wash.), Margaret M. Heckler (R Mass.), Marjorie S. Holt (R Md.), Elizabeth Holtzman (D N.Y.), Barbara C. Jordan (D Texas), Patsy T. Mink (D Hawaii), Leonor K. Sullivan (D Mo.), and Patricia Schroeder (D Colo.).

[8] "Seven Polarizing Issues in America Today," *The Annals of the American Academy of Political and Social Science,* September 1971, p. ix. The other issues were: military withdrawal from abroad, crackdown on crime, revenue sharing, White House vs. congressional power, 18-year-old vote, and regulation of pornography.

in at least 27 professional and academic associations.[9] *Science,* the journal of the American Association for the Advancement of Science, has taken up the cudgels for the women. "Male chauvinists would like to think that the current uproar is the work of a few militant troublemakers," *Science* said editorially on Jan. 14, 1971, in reference to anti-discrimination lawsuits brought by feminists against universities. "....The odds are, however, that we are witnessing a major movement that will persist until it has brought forth substantial changes...in the universities...[and] the professions."

Feminist threats of litigation to force the academic institutions to comply with anti-sex-discrimination provisions in the law have produced a real breakthrough. This was signified by the fact that the American Council on Education, the leading organization representing higher education in the nation, devoted its 1972 meeting to the woman question. Patricia Roberts Harris, a successful Washington lawyer, told the meeting that "women's liberation is the best thing that ever happened to higher education." Mrs. Harris, a former dean of Howard University Law School and ex-ambassador to Luxembourg, described the American university as "one of the most sexist institutions in the country."

Influence on News Media; Women's Magazines

Few social issues of the day have won more response from the news media than women's liberation. Lineage under the headings "woman" and "women" in *Readers' Guide,* an index of current periodicals, expanded as the movement swelled during the 1960s. Women's liberation and related issues became staples of Sunday supplement features and televised talk shows. A new class of celebrities from among women's liberation leaders was created. An unprecedented flow of books on the subject—polemics, scholarly analyses, sociological studies, revisionist histories, "new insight" revelations, and personal histories—poured from the presses. Few magazines of general circulation failed to feature articles on the phenomenon or to devote special issues or sections to "the new woman." Even *Esquire,* a man's magazine that once banned female authors, inaugurated a woman's column and devoted its July 1973 issue to women.

Vibrations from the movement reached the traditional women's magazines, influencing their content. Meanwhile,

---

[9] Among them: The American Association for the Advancement of Science, the American Association of Immunologists, the American Historical Association, the American Society of Biological Chemists, the Association of American Law Schools, the Modern Language Association, and the American Association of University Professors—all male bastions of professional eminence.

a proliferation of women's rights groups across the country accounted for a new growth of feminist broadsheets and newsletters. These provided, for the first time, a running account of what is happening of consequence to women's rights—action in the legislatures, in the courts, in women's organizations, the meetings and demonstrations, summaries of symposia and abstracts or listings of new books, articles and documents of various kinds. With such a profusion of documentation, it is not surprising that histories of the movement began to appear within a few years of its launching, some by women who had participated in the making of the history. Rarely had a movement told so much of its story as it went along.

Most ambitious of the new ventures in feminist publication is *Ms.* a slick monthly magazine put out by a corporation headed by Gloria Steinem, a feminist leader of striking good looks who is known, to her distaste, as the glamor girl of the movement. The founders of *Ms.* said they wanted "a publication created and controlled by women that could be as serious, outrageous, satisfying, sad, funky, intimate, global, compassionate, and full of change as women's lives really are." Despite the tremendous flow of words that had already been directed to the subject from every possible angle, *Ms.* felt "women just weren't getting serious or honest coverage."[10]

No end to the flow of feminist literature is in sight. Scholarship in feminist studies is a newly burgeoning field. New centers of women's studies, many based in universities, are providing new materials for formal study, for discussion, and for popularization in mass media. A history of the most recent phase of the feminist movement includes a 21-page bibliography; most of the citations are of recent vintage.

Dual Phases and Aims of Sexual-Equality Drive

The story they tell is of feminism moving along two tracks. One goes along the route of conventional action to achieve specific gains for women under the law and by reform of institutional practices. This is the feminism that lobbies, litigates and proselytizes for equal pay, for removal of sex discrimination in education and employment, for equal representation in political organizations. Conventional feminism also embraces a host of corollary "women's issues" such as provision of child-care facilities, tax reform that recognizes the economic value of homemaking, maternity leave provisions in labor con-

---

[10] "A Personal Report," *Ms.,* July 1972, pp. 4-7. *Ms.* first appeared as part of the December 1971 issue of *New York* magazine. A fuller so-called "Preview Edition," dated spring 1972, was distributed nationally in January 1972.

tracts, consumer protection, and so on.[11] Feminist pressure for goals of these kinds elicits fairly wide support from both sexes, even though entrenched practices to the contrary are slow to change.

The newer liberationist phase of the movement is more emotion-charged and controversial. It embraces a view of women as an exploited caste and attributes their exploitation to the power of social norms that have been established by men. Women, in this view, are victims not only because they have been relegated by law and custom to a secondary role which makes it hard for them to live as fully as men. The crowning victimization is that women have been conditioned to believe the secondary role is the right one for them. Convinced of their inferiority, the argument goes, many women fear to strike out for themselves beyond the protective if patronizing arm of the male. And even if they do seek to compete in the larger world, the male-dominated society has the cards stacked against them.

A primary goal of this newer form of feminism is to wake women up, make them explore their own experience as women and discover how it fits into the model of exploiter-exploited. Through the bond of sisterhood with fellow victims, it is hoped women will find courage to try to live on their own terms rather than in the shadow of the men in their lives. "We believe that only when millions of women all over the country are working directly to change their own lives will all of us be liberated from the oppression of a white, male-dominated society," wrote the founders of Women's Action Alliance in an undated "Dear Sisters" letter.

The two phases of feminism interlock at certain points, although their ideology and their tactics differ. The authors of a history of the movement write: "Although there has been cross-fertilization between the women's liberation and women's rights branches of the feminist movement, until 1970-71 there existed for all intents and purposes two movements distinct in their origins, politics, tactics, and general style.... Most of the moderate and conservative feminists...came from traditional...backgrounds: government work, state commissions on the status of women, women's business and professional groups. The women initially involved in the 'liberation' movement were generally younger...and came from a

---

[11] Abortion is one of these "women's issues," but one on which women are divided. The newer women's liberation movement, as distinct from the traditional feminist crusade, considers legalization (and lowering the price) of abortion central to the liberation of their sex.

more radical political background that had its roots in the student activism of the early 1960s."[12]

Although the liberation movement has been rent with frequent schisms and splinterings, it continues to draw new recruits including many who are only dimly aware of the doctrinal splits. "That despite this ignorance, small groups continue to form may well be a testament to the fact that the *idea* of women's liberation apparently touches a raw-nerve sensitivity in women regardless of their political orientation or lack of one," the authors state. The National Coalition for Research on Women's Education and Development, an organization of women in higher education founded in February 1971, would agree with that conclusion. "While women's frustrations are most vigorously aired by the women's liberation movement," the Coalition stated in a news release, March 26, 1971, "...investigations indicate that many adult women who shun strident protest share the beliefs...expressed [by the women's liberation movement.]"

Evolution of U.S. Women's Protest

WOMEN'S LIBERATION seemed to pop up out of nowhere, taking many people by surprise. Feminism had been considered, if not a dead issue, then at least a very minor one. With hindsight it now appears that the time was ripe for a feminist explosion. At the root of the movement were changes in the external conditions of daily life that were diminishing society's need to keep women confined to the domestic sphere and were drawing them increasingly into outside activities. The lowered birth rate, the marketing of convenience foods, the social acceptability of working mothers and the fact that a generation of girls had been raised with the idea that they ought to be able to "do something" with their lives besides keep house have all played a part in this.[13]

The climate of protest that pervaded the 1960s was ideal for the emergence of militant feminism in the manner and shape it took. Disillusionment with reform played its part among women's righters as it had with other aggrieved groups. Civil rights and welfare legislation had not remade the world for

---

[12] Judith Hole and Ellen Levine, *op. cit.* (1971), p. 109.
[13] See Elizabeth Janeway, *Man's World. Woman's Place* (1971).

the blacks and for the poor, and gains in women's rights had not lessened the feeling feminist women had of being at a disadvantage because of their sex. Their case against society apparently went too deep to be solved by mere changes in the rule book. Career women, college girls and young college-bred wives especially sensed a gap between what American society seemed to offer them and the actuality of their life situations.

Three pre-conditions necessary for the evolution of a protest movement came together at an opportune time for feminism, according to a male historian of the movement: "First a point of view around which to organize; second, a positive response by a portion of the aggrieved group; and third, a social atmosphere which is conducive to reform."[14] The "point of view" had been developing through the work of feminist scholars before the movement took hold of national consciousness. When the "social atmosphere" for protest was right, the aggrieved women responded to that "point of view" in the same manner that other protest groups had gained attention for their causes.

Analyses of Woman's Role as the 'Second Sex'

A major contribution to the development of a modern philosophy of women's liberation was *The Second Sex,* a scholarly and comprehensive study of the role of women in past and present by Simone de Beauvoir. This book, which first appeared in translation in the United States in 1952 three years after its publication in France, became a best-seller. It did not ignite an activist movement, but it did provide a "point of view" that held society responsible for committing woman to the role of "the other," secondary to man.

This concept is central to the women's liberation movement. De Beauvoir was not the first to enunciate it. A number of strong-minded women in the past, some of whose names are all but forgotten, had berated male-dominated society for denying women fuller expression of their gifts. The "Declaration of Sentiments and Resolutions" adopted at the first woman's rights convention at Seneca Falls in 1848 complained that "The history of mankind is a history of repeated injuries and usurpations on the part of man toward woman, having in direct object the establishment of an absolute tyranny over her." An early American feminist, Sarah Grimke, had said in 1837: "I ask no favor for my sex. All I ask of our brethren is that they take their feet off our necks."

---

[14] William Henry Chafe, *The American Woman* (1972), p. 227.

11

The value of the de Beauvoir work to feminist consciousness was that it covered every aspect of the woman question and provided an encyclopedia of scholarship to be mined by future feminist writers. *The Second Sex* was no polemic, but the general tone was one of regret for women's limited opportunities for fulfillment as human beings and it looked forward to a time when men and women, without denying their differences, could function as true equals.[15] Her last chapter was entitled "Toward Liberation."

The Second Sex was published during a quiescent period. The end of World War II had induced a back-to-the-home mood among American women. With their men returned from war service, women who had been the first of their sex to work in certain jobs in industry happily retired to domesticity. Some of them may have grown unhappy with the endless round of home-bound chores and they may have longed for a life beyond suburban housewifery, but little news of it got beyond the domestic circle.

Betty Friedan blew the whistle on the false paradise (at least for some women) with the publication of *The Feminine Mystique* in 1963. Friedan called on women to escape from the deadening enclosure of suburban domesticity and to seek a more fulfilling life as human beings, no longer to be mere servants to the needs of others. She did not decry the wife-mother roles, but pointed out that in modern times these did not offer enough scope for a healthy, intelligent woman. Like de Beauvoir before her, Friedan attacked the Freudian view that a woman is so psychologically subject to her sexual and reproductive functions that she is irretrievably destined to play a passive and retiring sex-determined role.[16] Also, like de Beauvoir, she deplored the conditioning of women, from little girlhood on, to acceptance of the passive role and dependence on male leadership. The result was said to convince women of their inferiority to men.

Friedan's book had a direct impact on the consciousness of women susceptible to its message. The birth control pill had promised a new freedom from unwanted childbirth and over-

---

[15] "To emancipate woman is to refuse to confine her to the relations she bears to man, not to deny them to her; let her have her independent existence and she will continue nonetheless to exist for him also; mutually recognizing each other as subject, each will yet remain for the other an *other.*—Simone de Beauvoir, *The Second Sex* (1952), p. 731.

[16] Freud wrote: "Women represent the interests of the family and of sexual life. The work of civilization has become increasingly the business of men; it confronts them with ever more difficult tasks and compels them to carry out instinctual sublimations of which women are little capable."—*Civilization and Its Discontents* (first published 1930) 1962 edition, James Strachey, trans., p. 50.

population was being regarded as the new menace. Postwar brides with children now reaching adolescence were no longer so enamored of simple domesticity while their daughters or younger sisters in college were getting caught up in movements that called for more personal self-expression in defiance of social custom. Both the suburban housewives who stayed home and those who returned to work felt the sting of the Friedan message.

After Friedan came a stream of books carrying her arguments into new realms. These led to an exploration of the sexual basis for woman's subjugation. The content of the polemics grew gamier, the tone angrier, the language more brutal. As if out to destroy the image of the "feminine" woman, more sensitive and delicate of spirit than men, hence in need of "protection" (read "subjugation"), women's lib authors struck out against male sexuality in the language of barroom brawlers. Norman Mailer, known to the movement as the arch example of the sexist male, expressed shock at the language. "A few of the women were writing in a way no women had ever written before...," he wrote.[17] "It was...a mean style."

Some not only turned against the institution of marriage but decried the love relationship itself as an enslavement. They would be as tough about sex as men were. This trend in women's lib caused considerable concern among more moderate groups. When a Lesbian faction emerged, the alienations within the movement were almost as sharp as those with non-liberationist society.

Founding of Activist Groups to Attack Sex Bias

Interest stirred by her book led Betty Friedan and others to found The National Organization of Women (Now) in 1966 to serve as an activist group for bringing pressure on government, industry and other agencies to terminate sex discrimination. Now's statement of purpose, announced at a press conference in October 1966, presented a classic feminist position. In the spectrum of current feminist doctrine, it is a relatively conservative platform. It does not call for radical change in the performance of women's traditional functions and it welcomes men as partners in reform.[18]

---

[17] Norman Mailer, *The Prisoner of Sex* (1971), pp. 39-40.

[18] There are male members of Now, inviting comparison with the white membership of such organizations as The National Association for the Advancement of Colored People (NAACP). Like the more radical black organizations, the more radical women's liberationist groups argue that the oppressed must fight for liberation without help from sympathizers from the ranks of the "oppressor." This is one of many instances of the similarity of doctrinal structure and language between the women's liberation and the black liberation movements.

It is no longer either necessary or possible [the statement continued] for women to devote the greater part of their lives to child-rearing....

We do not accept the traditional assumption that a woman has to choose between marriage and motherhood on the one hand and serious participation in industry or the professions on the other....

We believe that a true partnership between the sexes demands a different concept of marriage, an equitable sharing of the responsibilities of home and children and of the economic burdens of their support.

Now promised to try to change "the false image of women now prevalent in the mass media and in the texts, ceremonies, laws and practices of our major social institutions." It thought "such images perpetuate contempt for women by society and by women for themselves."[19]

Persistence of the Movement Despite Divisions

It was as participants in protest movements dedicated to other causes that young women activists were led to develop a newer brand of feminism known as women's liberation. These were the young women who crusaded for civil rights for blacks and other minorities, who demonstrated against the war in Vietnam, supported draft resistance, and were drawn into various liberal or "new left" movements. Though these movements were generally dedicated to an egalitarian ideal and opposed the prevailing "power structure," the women found that they were no less victims of sexist oppression in their groups than they were in the larger society. If the suburban housewife was saddled with housework and child care while her husband enjoyed lordly status and personal satisfaction in the larger world, or if the working wife had to bear the double burden of job and housework with little gain of status, the women of the liberal and radical movements were no less demeaned by being relegated to making coffee and typing while the male members decided policy and led the action.

This phase of the liberation movement began in the form of women's caucuses within the male-dominated activist groups. According to one "insider" account, an effort to bring up women's rights issues at a Students for a Democratic Society (SDS) conference in December 1965 elicited catcalls and verbal abuse and the following year SDS women who demanded a women's lib plank were pelted with tomatoes and thrown out of the convention.[20]

---

[19] See "Marriage: Changing Institution," *E.R.R.*, 1971 Vol. II, pp. 761-777.

[20] Marlene Dixon, "One Woman's Liberation," *Radical America*, February 1970, p. 27.

The first women's lib group to be formed independently of the male-dominated organizations began as a seminar on women's issues at a free university program at the University of Chicago in 1967. Realizing that men in the liberal and radical movements were no more ready to accept women as equals than men in the establishment world, the women decided to strike out on a feminist struggle of their own. The idea caught on and small groups began to form in other cities and university towns. But there was no unifying creed beyond the general liberationist orientation and there were splinterings even within the small groups that did form. Nevertheless, despite these organizational handicaps, the women of the movement succeeded in raising the consciousness of the nation on an issue that only a few years ago was thought to have been laid away in mothballs. And they did this at a time when a half-dozen other issues, based on the grievances of other segments of the population, were fighting for attention. How did they do it? Their major instrument was "consciousness-raising."

Consequences of Consciousness Raising

THE TERM "consciousness raising" did not originate with women's liberation but it has become so integral a part of the movement that it is hard to disassociate the two. Consciousness raising on the feminist issue has been achieved by three means: by numerous studies and interpretations of the female condition in American society, by public acts designed to attract attention in the news media, and by "rap sessions," that is, the exchange of personal confidences of women in small-group meetings.

Writings of latter-day feminists have provided the philosophic underpinnings of the movement and constitute a basic resource for the endless debates on various aspects of the woman question. This new body of feminist literature differs markedly from that of the past in style and content. It goes into subjects, such as the differences between vaginal and clitoral orgasm, that would have shocked feminists of the past—and left them confused as to the relevance to women's rights. Nevertheless, the shock value of contemporary feminist writings had much to do with "spreading the word" that a new day was dawning for women's rights. Perhaps the most shocking of all women's lib books is Ellen Frankfort's *Vaginal Politics* (1972), an attack on the medical profession's treatment of female patients.

Numerous demonstrations served to widen the range of recognition of the movement beyond the immediately affected circle. Some of these actions—picketing and sit-ins— had a specific objective, as when the women protested a particular form of sex discrimination. But many of the actions were taken primarily to "raise women's consciousness of their societal oppression and reveal men to themselves as oppressors."[21]

Much of what seemed silliest or most outrageous in women's lib activism was a form of "street theater," a tactic borrowed from other protest movements for gaining attention to the cause. The so-called bra-burning episode, for example, did as much as anything in liberation activism to push the movement to the forefront of national consciousness. In fact, bras were not burned. The occasion was a protest on Sept. 7, 1968, against the Miss America beauty contest at Atlantic City, which the protesters denounced as one of the many ways society demeans women. A group of women threw undergarments, hair rollers, and high-heel shoes into a trash can—discarding symbols of the male ideal of feminine allure.

Small-Group Exchanges of Personal Testimony

The small-group talk session is the activity to which the term consciousness raising is most often applied. These sessions are akin to those held by participants in encounter groups.[22] Consicousness-raising sessions in the women's liberation movement were staged when it was realized that by talking together in small groups, women begin to recognize their shared disabilities and thus discover the relevance of the liberation movement to their own situation. The process of giving testimony within a small trusted group was found to be an effective prelude to radicalizing or politicizing an individual woman's vague discontent with her lot in life. "The collective thinking that is characteristic of the feminist movement is built on the feeling of identity with all women that consciousness raising gives."[23]

In time a rough set of rules developed, with some variations depending on the group. *Ms.* has described the proper proce-

---

[21] Cellestine Ware, *Woman Power: The Movement for Women's Liberation* (1970), p. 130.
[22] See "Encounter Groups," *E.R.R.*, 1971 Vol. I, pp. 165-186.
[23] Ware, *op. cit.*, p. 138.

dures of the "intimate and supportive talk sessions" that are "the heart and soul of the women's movement." The group must be small, at most 15, with optimum size 6 to 10. No men must be present, not even well-meaning ones ("If the men want to help let them stay home and mind the kids"). Meetings are usually held in a member's home once a week and each lasts two to four hours. Each woman, in turn, is given a chance to talk freely without fear of being challenged by any other. This encourages the women to speak out. "The result is that things are said that might never otherwise emerge in group discussion.... For many women, it is the first time they have ever been listened to seriously by a group."[24]

The consciousness-raising "rap sessions" have met a certain amount of criticism within the movement—that they tend to degenerate into self-indulgent repetitions of personal griev-ances. "It gets boring to listen to someone else always talking about their problems," a participant complained. "...after [one girl] talked about her depression everyone got tired of hearing about it."[25] The problem is to move from conscious-ness raising to political action. One radical feminist com-plained that "the length of time spent on this one aspect of revolution is so extended that some women know nothing else about feminism after months in the movement."[26]

"The problem with consciousness raising," wrote another feminist, "is that discoveries are made, yes.... But what is one to *do* with them?.... A new idea about oneself...unsettles all one's other ideas.... No matter how slightly, it shifts one's en-tire orientation. And somewhere along the line...it changes one's behavior."[27] Consciousness raising according to a femin-ist psychologist, has made some women "happier, angrier, more confident, more adventurous, more moral."

> Some women [she continued] quit their jobs...others began job training.... Some women started living together; some began living alone for the first time... Some women left their husbands; others began to live with a man, feeling somehow less of a psychological disadvantage than before....

> "Many women started reading 'political' and 'scientific' books as passionately as they read novels.... Within a small group... women stopped giggling and competing with each other for male attention.... Many women found they could think.... Some women stopped going to beauty parlors.... [They] began to value their

---

[24] "A Guide to Consciousness Raising," *Ms.*, July 1972, pp. 18-23.
[25] Quoted by Phyllis Chesler, *Women & Madness* (1972), p. 260.
[26] Jeanne Arrow, "Danger in the Pro-Women Line and Consciousness Raising," quoted by Ware, *op. cit.*, p. 111.
[27] Patricia McLaughlin, "Comment," *The American Scholar*, autumn 1972, p. 622.

time; they needed fewer adornments to "make up" for being female."[28]

Women's liberation, in both its relatively conservative and its more radical orientations, has been largely a movement of well-educated, middle-class white women. Black women have not been entirely aloof from the movement, however, although their feminism is deeply enmeshed in their feelings about racism. In a talk before the staff of the U.S. Commission on Civil Rights in December 1972, Margaret Sloan of the *Ms.* staff said: "All over the country there are black groups and women's groups that have gotten together." Black household workers who press for better pay and working conditions "very clearly [are] making the connection between their lives and the women's movement," she said.

Question of Reaching Beyond White Middle Class

Further indications of the movement's spreading beyond its original nuclei were given in a recent account of consciousness raising among middle-aged wives of blue-collar workers in Brooklyn. These were home-bound women at a time of life when their children were leaving home and they were feeling at a loss about their futures. "The women...identify with the movement on a variety of specific issues—child day-care centers, equal pay for equal work, the right to abortion and contraceptive information, the need to educate young girls to think of themselves as individuals in their own right instead of viewing themselves only as future wives and mothers," writes Susan Jacoby. As a result of consciousness-raising group meetings, some of the women took jobs, some went back to school and some pressed on their husbands the importance of college educations for daughters as well as sons.[29]

The women's liberation movement has influenced men sympathetic to the cause and now there are male consciousness-raising sessions dedicated to "human liberation." The idea is that men are victimized by society's demand that they conform to the male stereotype, which means they must be aggressive, competitive, suppress tender feelings, prove their virility by sexual conquest, and get ahead—a conditioning that leads to ulcers, heart trouble, unhappy marriages, and premature death. "There are signs throughout the country that men are beginning to embrace the feminist revolution as their own cause," writes Russ Rueger, sociologist at the

---

[28] Phyllis Chesler, *Women & Madness* (1972), pp. 243-4.
[29] Susan Jacoby, "Feminism in the $12,000-a-year family: 'What do I do for the next 20 years?'" *The New York Times Magazine,* June 17, 1973, pp. 17, 49.

University of California at Irvine. "It might be an overstatement to call these efforts a 'movement' at present but...there have been many...attempts in widespread areas...an indication that men's liberation may be answering a grass-roots need."[30] Warren Farrell, author of *Beyond Masculinity*, who teaches at Rutgers University, has launched at least 20 men's consciousness-raising groups around the country. He heads a task force of Now which plans to stimulate a further growth in the coming year.

Paying the Price for Full Equality of the Sexes

During discussion of plans for a special edition on feminism, a woman member of the board of *The American Scholar* posed the question—"If we win, what do we lose?" The question exasperated the seven professionally successful women invited by the publication to participate in a discussion of women's liberation. But the question has real meaning for many women who cling to the traditional pattern of woman the homemaker and man the supporter and protector of the home. Women liberationists were taken off-guard when opposition to the movement took the form of organized protests by ad hoc groups of women against the Equal Rights Amendment, contributing to the defeat of ratification in some states.

Midge Decter, a severe critic of the movement, claims most women would not want to pay the price of the freedom envisioned by the liberationists. The movement's basic premise is wrong, she claims; women are *not* victimized by male-dominated society. What makes women unhappy today is not that they are confined to a limited role in life but that they have freedom to choose their roles and are afraid to make the choice. "For women to claim that they are victims when they are so clearly not is merely an expression of their terror in the face of the harshness and burdens of new and as yet not fully claimed freedom," she writes. "The plain unvarnished fact is that every woman wants to marry. She may want in addition to be a doctor or a lawyer.... But...she will want as a basic pinning for her life to be married.... She requires both in her nature and by virtue of what are her immediate practical needs...the assurance that a single man has undertaken to love, cherish and support her."

The most sweeping condemnation of the new feminism is conveyed in an article based on a forthcoming book by George Gilder in the June 1973 issue of *Harper's*. Gilder warns that if

---

[30] "Men's Lib," *Human Behavior*, April 1973, p. 75.

the movement should succeed, it would spell the destruction of true, lasting love in marriage and that society generally and women specifically would suffer as a result. "The differences between the sexes are the single most important fact of human society," he writes. "The drive to deny them— in the name of women's liberation,...must be one of the most quixotic crusades in the history of the species." He carries his objections even to the point of approving higher pay for men workers on the ground that their social role requires an economic advantage. "A woman with more money than [the] men around her tends to demoralize them.... She weakens their connections with the community and promotes a reliance upon other anti-social ways of confirming their masculinity...."[31]

A more sympathetic male observer, William Henry Chafe, history professor at Duke University, points out that the movement's consciousness-raising activities have come at a time when social conditions are changing in favor of feminist goals. "Important shifts in behavior have taken place and the changes bear directly on some of the root causes of sexual inequality, the definition of male and female spheres, the role models we provide our children, the permissible horizons available to men and women." If women and especially married women are to sustain sufficient commitment to the pursuit of careers then they "must be guided by a high degree of ideological energy and awareness," writes Chafe, and the movement "can help to provide that energy."[32]

The continuing flow of married women into the job market may be the key to the change. A Labor Department study showed that as of March 1972, 35 per cent of all families "headed by married men" included a working wife; the future seems to point to a more active role for women outside the home. Looking back, the future historian may see consciousness raising of women's liberation not so much as an agent of change as a reaction to an invincible tide of change.

---

[31] George Gilder, "The Suicide of the Sexes," *Harper's*, June 1973, pp. 42-54.
[32] William Henry Chafe, *op. cit.*, pp. 252-253.

MARRIAGE: CHANGING INSTITUTION

by

Helen B. Shaffer

WEAKENING OF MONOGAMOUS STANDARD
Forces Buffeting Marriage in Modern Society
Views on Whether Marriage is Sick or Dying
Premarital Sex; Vanishing Ideal of Virgin Bride
Mate Swapping Among Middle-Class Couples

MARRIAGE AND WESTERN CIVILIZATION
Social Pressure in Ancient Societies to Marry
Growth of Ecclesiastic Control Over Marriage
Marriage Contracts Engineered by Patriarchs
Late Linking of Romantic Love With Marriage
Marriage and Divorce Laws in the United States

VISIONS OF THE FUTURE OF MARRIAGE
Attention Directed to Saving Modern Marriages
Effect of Sex-Charged Environment on Monogamy
Multiple Variations Seen as Pattern of the Future

1971
Oct. 6

MARRIAGE: CHANGING INSTITUTION

S O MANY ODD AND CONTRARY forces are pressing on marriage in America today that only one conclusion is supportable: The venerable institution of matrimony must be undergoing momentous change. No one at this point can be sure what will become of it. Many forces are buffeting marriage about. The sexual revolution is bringing on a widening acceptance of premarital, extramarital and group sex. Contraception that is almost foolproof is freeing women from the "biological trap" within and outside of marriage. The women's liberation movement and the economic independence of many women are creating pressure for redefining male and female roles.

Americans are encouraged in a multitude of ways to cast off restraints imposed by traditional moral codes governing marriage. Old taboos are breaking down as to out-of-wedlock births and homosexual mating. Notions of fidelity in marriage seem quaint in today's literature or on its movie and television screens. Moreover, many traditional functions of the family have been shifted to the state or other impersonal institutions, thus diminishing the social necessity of marriage. The new emphasis on leisure as a life goal tends to blur or erase the old concept in marriage of the husband as the breadwinner and the wife as the homemaker. Additionally, the cults of individualism and anti-institutionalism have caused some young people to reject the legalization of marriage. Beyond that, the high divorce rate feeds a growing skepticism about the permanence of love in marriage.

The list could be longer. What it adds up to is change. But where will it all end? Some say marriage is doomed, at least as Americans have long conceived it; that is, as a legally and spiritually or religiously sanctioned monogamous relationship, involving a mutual commitment of love and fidelity between two persons who have a reasonable expectation that the union will endure until death. Marriage is also conceived as a social institution imposing certain obligations and granting certain rights to each partner. Their sharing extends to matters economic, psychic, sexual and parental.

"The total institution of marriage in American society is gravely ill," write Rustum and Della Roy, a married couple, both scientists, parents of three, and co-authors of a book entitled *Honest Sex* (1969). Though conceding that "millions of Americans have sound marriages in which they have found love and mutual satisfaction," the Roys say their research has shown monogamous marriage in the United States to be "enveloped by deterioration and decay," and the source of much unhappiness. They cite a study indicating that in some West Coast communities "75 per cent of marriages are a 'bust.' "[1]

Views on Whether Marriage is Sick or Dying

Sociologists have written at length on the "breakdown" of the Negro family. The Moynihan Report in 1965 stated: "Nearly a quarter of urban Negro marriages are dissolved; nearly one-quarter of Negro births are now illegitimate; as a consequence, almost one-fourth of Negro families are now illegitimate."[2] Moynihan found the root of the problem in slavery and the position of the Negro man in an urban setting—the "last hired and first fired." Moynihan's views have been debated and assailed, especially by Negro leaders. But now, in the year 1971, the focus on family deterioration has shifted to a broader stage, away from a racial context.

The women's liberation movement has spawned a small army of female authors echoing the plaint of the French feminist, Simone de Beauvoir, who argued nearly a generation ago that marriage was an oppressive institution for men and women, but especially for women.[3] A large accumulation of recent "literature" on the subject of marriage is heavily weighted with advice on how to keep it from going sour. Where so many prescriptions for cure are offered, it would seem that some pathology must be present. "Calamity always attracts

---

[1] Rustum and Della Roy, "Is Monogamy Outdated?" *The Humanist,* March-April 1970, p. 19.

[2] *The Negro Family: The Case for National Action,* written by a governmental task force headed by Daniel Patrick Moynihan, a sociologist and author who was then Assistant Secretary of Labor in the Johnson administration. Non-white families headed by females rose to almost 29 per cent in 1971, according to government statistics; the figure for white families remained relatively unchanged at 9 per cent.

[3] Simone de Beauvoir, *The Second Sex* (Bantam edition, 1961), p. 454. *The Second Sex* was first published in France in 1949, and in the United States in 1953. The author, now 63, never married but has maintained a 40-year relationship with Jean-Paul Sarte. See Curtis Cate, "Europe's First Feminist Has Changed the Second Sex," *The New York Times Magazine,* July 11, 1971, p. 5.

MARITAL STATUS OF AMERICANS, 18 AND OLDER

Status	Male (in thousands)	Male (in percentages)	Female (in thousands)	Female (in percentages)
Single	11,894	19.0	9,536	13.7
Married, living with spouse*	45,036	72.2	44,888	64.6
Married, spouse absent**	1,711	2.7	2,719	3.7
Widowed	2,110	3.4	9,639	13.8
Divorced	1,577	2.5	2,693	3.6
Totals†	62,329	100.00	69,474	100.00

*Difference in numbers as to wives and husbands is due to the fact that more wives than husbands are under 18 years of age.

**Figures include legal separations and other categories, including husbands away from home on military duty.

†Figures may not add to totals because of rounding.

SOURCE: Adapted from Census Bureau data.

---

attention," write the authors of a recent book on marriage problems, "and in the United States the state of marriage is a calamity."[4]

There still are optimists who consider some of the changes taking place as supportive of marriage. According to this view, the only loss is a shucking off of hypocrisy and meaningless ceremony. The changes are said to point to a more honest and equitable relationship between men and women as love mates and greater security for children no longer victimized by the neuroses of parents locked in an oppressive marital union. Even the extraordinary phenomenon of mate swapping and group sex among married couples is viewed by some as a safeguard of the marital relationship.

But whether the future for marriage looks bright or baleful, the factor of rapid change—more rapid even than in the immediate past—seems inescapable. Alvin Toffler emphasized in his book *Future Shock* (1970) that the accelerating pace of change is unsettling in all circumstances of human life. It is not to be wondered that marriage and the family would be caught in the change speed-up. "As conventional marriage proves itself less and less capable of delivering on its promise of lifelong love...we can anticipate public acceptance of temporary marriages," Toffler wrote. While Americans may yearn for a permanent relationship, he added, "something inside whispers to them that it is an increasingly improbable

---

[4] W. H. Lederer and Don D. Jackson, *The Mirages of Marriage* (1968), p. 13.

luxury." A newspaper reporter wrote, after traveling around the Unived States for six months that he had found many Americans "rejecting the rigid moral positions of the past, whether on abortion or extramarital affairs or 'aberrant' sexual behavior."[5]

Premarital Sex; Vanishing Ideal of Virgin Bride

Today the taboo on sex before marriage appears to be falling away fast. Of course there is no way of comparing actual incidence of premarital sex of today with that of past eras. Surveys of sex experience are a form of research peculiar to this age. What seems clear and significant is that the shame of premarital sex is disappearing, while affirmation of it as a positive value is gaining ground. Not only are more young women discarding the old moral code concerning virginity, but an increasing number of young people, as Margaret Mead noted several years ago, clamor "for a new morality that will put a seal of approval on premarital sex."[6]

When Dr. Alfred C. Kinsey reported in 1953 on his studies of sexual behavior of American women, many readers were startled to discover that more than 50 per cent of the women he studied had had premarital sexual intercourse. The younger the generation, the more likely it was that sexual relations took place before marriage. The Kinsey reports on the sexual habits of American men and women[7] broke the taboo on scientific inquiry in this field. Since then research into sexual practices, in and out of marriage, has grown rapidly—in itself a reflection of changing mores affecting marital relations.

A survey of sociological studies conducted during the past decade about premarital intercourse showed a rising curve both in actual performance and in openness of mind about it. "Apparently there is not a single major study that has been made in the late 1960s that has found premarital coital rates that were the level of those found in the late 1950s or early 1960s," the authors of the survey wrote.[8] They noted, in particular, "a substantial increase in feminine approval of premarital coitus and experience therewith." The focus of

---

[5] Haynes Johnson, *The Washington Post*, July 4, 1971. See also "Sexual Revolution: Myth or Reality," *E.R.R.*, 1970 Vol. I, pp. 241-258, and "Abortion Law Reform," *E.R.R.*, 1970 Vol. II, pp. 545-562.

[6] "Margaret Mead Answers Questions," *Redbook*, March 1968, p. 10.

[7] Alfred C. Kinsey, Wardell B. Pomeroy, and Clyde E. Martin, *Sexual Behavior in the Human Male* (1948), and the same authors with Paul H. Gebhard, *Sexual Behavior in the Human Female* (1953).

[8] Kenneth L. Cannon and Richard Long, "Premarital Sex Behavior in the Sixties," *Journal of Marriage and the Family*, February 1971, pp. 39-40.

research had shifted in one respect: There was declining interest in the question of whether losing virginity before marriage harmed the prospect of happiness in marriage. The few studies concerned with this question indicated that either there was no effect or a beneficial one.

A significant difference was found between recent studies and those of a few years earlier. The earlier studies showed that the non-virginal bride had usually had sexual relations with only one man before marriage, and that he was the man she married. While this practice did not abide by the conventional wisdom of the advice-from-the-lovelorn columnists, it seemed to present little threat to the ideal of monogamous marriage since the premarital relationship was exclusive and apparently regarded as a prelude to legal marriage.

The more recent studies show rising rates of sexual intercourse among young women without regard to expectations of marriage. Female students surveyed in 1968 at an urban university disclosed that of those who had premarital coitus, only 19 per cent had first experienced it while they were engaged to be married. Fully three-fourths had first experienced sexual intercourse in a dating relationship—not necessarily even a "going steady" dating relationship. Many of these young women not only felt no necessity of having a commitment of marriage, they felt no remorse. This could "indicate the first significant change in premarital sexual behavior patterns since the 1920s," the survey authors commented in reporting their findings.[9]

A Gallup poll conducted on 55 campuses in the spring of 1970 showed that three-fourths of the students questioned said virginity was not an important consideration in the person they would marry. An equal proportion of males and females responding to this question felt that way. The poll tended to confirm what other studies have indicated: that virginity becomes less and less valued as the student progresses up the class ladder—68 per cent of the freshmen but 80 per cent of the seniors and 83 per cent of the graduate students did not value virginity in a prospective mate.[10] Although these figures applied only to college students, the

---

[9] Robert R. Bell and Jay B. Chaskes, "Premarital Sexual Experience Among Coeds, 1958 and 1968," *Journal of Marriage and Family*, February 1970, p. 84. Those who had experienced intercourse during a dating situation rose from 10 per cent in 1958 to 23 per cent in 1968, the authors reported.

[10] The generation gap is indicated by the results of a Gallup poll taken in August 1969. Sixty-eight per cent of the adults who were questioned said premarital sex was wrong.

43228

influence of this segment of the youth population on the attitudes and values of youth generally is widely apparent. The
influence of campus manners and morals is especially notice-
able among high school students. But there are other signs
indicating that a weakening of the moral code guarding
monogamous marriage has moved beyond the youth culture
to reach the very citadel of conventionality—the suburban
married couple.

Mate Swapping Among Middle-Class Couples

Mate swapping has been portrayed recently as an activity
of growing popularity among married couples. No one knows
how far the practice has actually spread. Estimates as to the
number of American couples who participate—"swing"—range
from one million to eight million. Marriage counselors report
their clients increasingly make reference to swinging. A
number of magazines appealing to a swinger readership have
appeared and apparently are prospering. Of particular signif-
icance is that recruits to swinging are being drawn from a
very solid element of middle-class America. A number of
research teams in the academic world have considered swinging a subject worthy of serious study. Their studies indicate
that the largest concentration of swingers is in the San Francisco and Los Angeles areas. The New York-Boston-Washing-
ton megalopolis is a close second and the Chicago area is third.

Swinging may take a number of forms. Two married couples may meet, agree on their compatibility, and simply exchange partners for a brief sexual episode. Or a number
of couples may come together for a party, with the under-
standing that partners will be reshuffled for sexual encounters.
These may take place either in private or in the company of
other sex partners. Or the party may be a sexual free-for-all.
Voyeurism appears to be a significant part of swinging.

Mate swapping was not exactly unknown in the past and in
some cultures the loan of a wife is an expected gesture of
hospitality. But it is doubtful whether the search for sexual
variety in marriage had ever before become organized to
the degree described by Gilbert D. Bartell in *Group Sex: A
Scientist's Eyewitness Report on the American Way of
Swinging,* published early in 1971. Bartell, a professor of
anthropology at Northern Illinois University, investigated
group swinging with the aid of his wife over a period of years.[11]

---

[11] Their research is said to come from witnessing and interviewing, not from
participating.

The enterprise he describes is comparable in its requirements for organizational expertise to that of running a successful business or civic club.

A man and wife who want to swing place carefully worded ads in appropriate publications to attract interested couples. The couples chosen must be of the right type for there is little crossing of class or age lines. Meetings or social get-togethers are arranged to size up prospective participants and weed out the unpromising. All of this entails considerable correspondence, exchange of pictures, long-distance telephoning, and travel. The effort is all the more difficult because it must be clandestine. Neighbors must not know what is going on and children must be sent off to sleep elsewhere. Attention to detail is important. The menstrual cycles of the participating women, for example, must be taken into consideration in setting party dates. Even if swingers' clubs take care of arrangements, as they sometimes do, participating in swinging as described by Dr. Bartell consumes time and energy. Some couples drop out for that reason.

Swinging in the suburbs is hemmed in by conventions and taboos which sustain the aspect of decorum to be expected at any proper social event. Participants must be well-dressed, sociable and well-mannered. No crudities of speech or behavior will be tolerated. Extremely high standards of personal hygiene are demanded. There must be no ruckus. No one is forced to participate, but if one member refuses, his spouse must refuse also. Some of the rules are intended to prevent marital discord. The sexual encounter must not lead to emotional involvement. Couples who come together are expected to leave together. Mates are not supposed to show jealousy. To preserve the impersonality of sex in swinging, the same sets of couples rarely swing with one another more than once or twice. Therefore a couple that wants to continue swinging must be on a constant search for new collaborators.

The swingers described by Dr. Bartell were conventional by all standards but that of sexual habits. Aside from swinging, the women's interests were confined mainly to homemaking and children; their husbands talked of sports and taxes. Their politics was conservative. Not all swingers follow this pattern, however. Some scorn the organizational network. They simply swing with their friends. For them the taboo on emotional involvement is reversed: They are revolted at the idea of going to bed with a stranger or of having sex without affection.

Marriage and Western Civilization

THE ORIGINS of marriage are lost in the speculations of anthropologists. "Marriage is older than man," historian Will Durant wrote, noting the matrimonial habits of lower primates.[12] During the upheavals in scientific thinking and method a century ago, a new school of investigators into the prehistoric past dismissed the prevailing belief in primeval monogamy as a myth.[13] After that, authorities argued the question back and forth from the meager data at their disposal. Today it is generally accepted that the earliest kind of mating to form a family was probably polygyny—one man with several wives.[14]

This view is based partly on the assumption that there was an excess of females in primeval times, due to the hazards to the male of the hunt. And it is based partly on evidence of polygyny in early nomadic and primitive agricultural societies, suggesting a carryover from an even more remote past. The question comes down to whether there is an instinctual preference in man for monogamy. The evidence leans rather to the negative. Monogamous marriage was apparently the creation of man at a relatively late stage of development.

Monogamy appeared, obviously, to meet certain social needs. But it also created a host of biological problems. Bertrand Russell expressed envy of the anthropoid apes because, once mated, they ceased to be sexually attracted to any but their mates. "Among the anthropoid apes,...although they do not have the assist of religion, sin is unknown, since instinct suffices to produce virtue."[15]

Social Pressure in Ancient Societies to Marry

Modern marriage in the West descends from the early Judaic model, modified by the Christian ideal and numerous social forces acting on it over the years. The ancient Hebrews had many wives, as the Bible attests, and the practice was not

---

[12] Will Durant, *The Story of Civilization: Part I, Our Oriental Heritage* (1935), p. 37.

[13] Bronislaw Malinowski, article in the British magazine *Nature*, April 22, 1922, reprinted in his book *Sex, Culture, and Myth* (1962), p. 117.

[14] Polygyny is distinguished from polyandry (more than one husband per wife) and polygamy (multiple mates for either spouse).

[15] Bertrand Russell, *"Marriage and Morals"* (1957 edition of 1929 publication), p. 131.

abolished until well into the Christian era.[16] But from ancient times the Jews extolled marriage as the ideal form of human mating. They encouraged it at any early age—as young as 12 for girls and 13 for boys—and bound it with rules designed to preserve its dignity, stability and permanence. Hebrew society had little place for unmarried adults; everyone was expected to marry. Jewish law provided for remarriage of a widow to the brother of the deceased.

The Greeks forbade single blessedness. Sexual fidelity in marriage, however, was another story. Sparta denied the franchise to bachelors, but encouraged extramarital intercourse if it was likely to produce exceptionally vigorous offspring. Demosthenes may have indicated the degree to which the Greeks adhered to the monogamous ideal in the fourth century B.C. when he said: "We have courtesans for the sake of pleasure, concubines for the daily health of our bodies, and wives to bear us lawful offspring and be the faithful guardians of our homes."

Early Roman society, organized around kinship groups, had little place for single persons. Men married early and divorce, as with the Jews, was restricted. Husbands were permitted to execute a wife caught in adultery, although a similar privilege did not accrue to the wife. As Rome prospered, the hold of traditional moral codes weakened and marriage foundered. By the time of Emperor Augustus (63 B.C.-14 A.D.) many Romans were avoiding marriage, preferring to consort only with prostitutes and concubines, while the married lived gaily and sought to avoid childbirth.[17] Augustus hoped to restore respect for the old morality by enacting laws to encourage and stabilize marriage and to re-emphasize its reproductive function. The laws penalized the celibate, even the widowed who did not remarry, as well as those married persons who had few or no children.

Growth of Ecclesiastic Control Over Marriage

The early Christians broke with the past by their glorification of celibacy. From St. Paul onward, the early Church Fathers made it clear that marriage was second best and that to remain virginal was the way of life most pleasing to Christ.

---

[16] Rabbi Gershom ben Judah of Mainz, about the year 1000, decreed excommunication of polygamous Jews. "Soon thereafter, in all Europe except Spain, polygamy and concubinage became almost extinct among the Jews."—Will Durant, *The Story of Civilization: Part IV, The Age of Faith* (1950), p. 380.

[17] Various unguents and procedures, including *coitus interruptus,* were used for contraception in the ancient world.

Paul's first epistle (Corinthians 7:7-9) urged bachelors to avoid fornication "but if they cannot contain, let them marry: for it is better to marry than to burn." Thus while the Roman emperors were penalizing men and women who failed to establish families, Christianity was praising those who avoided matrimony. "Not only was great merit attached to abstention from marriage and from sexual intercourse, but special prestige belonged to those who pledged themselves to lifelong celibacy. In no other culture have we found anything like this."[18]

Despite its lauding of celibacy, the Church recognized the necessity of marriage and sought to gain control over it. A body of rules and regulations, derived from various edicts, pronouncements and judgments, became codified eventually in the form of canon law. The anti-sex bias of the church was often manifested. The fourth Council of Carthage in 398, for example, ruled that a newly married couple should spend their first night as virgins "out of reverence for the benediction"—a rule later mitigated. Celibacy of the clergy was affirmed by the 11th century.

The Church gradually injected itself as a third party—the officiating agency—in the marriage ceremony. Until then marriage, although governed by certain laws and religious customs, was essentially a private contract, requiring neither civil magistrate nor priest as officiator. The ceremony varied with the different cultures, but its basic requirements had been the pledging of the terms of the marital contract before witnesses and the consummation of the union. The Church at first added a benediction; then the couple was required to attend a mass. Later special phrases were introduced taking cognizance of the marriage, and then a formal liturgy for the wedding ceremony was adopted. By the ninth century some churchmen considered marriage a sacrament, but it was not until the Council of Trent (1545-63) that the Church formally affirmed marriage as one of the seven sacraments.

Marriage Contracts Engineered by Patriarchs

Though marriage has always been essentially a contractual agreement between two parties, during much of the past the contracting parties were not the bride and groom but their fathers. Patriarchal power governed choice in marriage from

---

[18] Stuart A. Queen and John B. Adams, *The Family in Various Cultures* (1952), p. 157.

the earliest biblical era almost up to modern times. Paternal control of the choice of principals and of the terms of the marriage contract underlined the economic aspects of the union.

The economic value of wives in agricultural society was indicated by the early practice of setting a purchase price for a bride. The price might be property or labor. Jacob, for example, served Laban 14 years to win first Leah, then Rachel, for wife. In later centuries, both a dower and a dowry were required. The dower was a sum or property set aside for the wife in case she were to be abandoned or widowed; the dowry was a gift from the bride's father to the bridegroom. The dower and the dowry continued to figure prominently in the marriage contract through the ages and there are still vestiges of it in modern marriage.

Late Linking of Romantic Love With Marriage

Romantic love or sexual passion as the main basis for marriage is a relatively recent development. History, myth, and the arts of the past are replete with evocations of ardent love affairs, but the affairs rarely pertained to connubial bliss.

> Romantic love—i.e., love that idealizes its object—probably occurred in every age, in degree loosely corresponding with the delay and obstacles between desire and fulfillment. Until our own age it was rarely the cause of marriage; and if we find it quite apart from marriage when knighthood was in flower, we must view that condition as more normal than our own.[19]

Romantic love in the modern age is traced back to the age of chivalry which began in southern France in the 10th century, then spread across Europe to reach its peak in the 13th century. The chivalric tradition grew out of conditions in the feudal manor, where the high-born ladies played games of love with young squires and troubadors while their husbands were off fighting. It was a major tenet of the chivalric code that love out of marriage was superior to that in marriage, because the former was given freely while the latter was given as a matter of duty. "Courts of love" at that time even denied that true love could exist in marriage.

Marriage customs in the age of chivalry made little allowance for romance and a great deal for economics and, among the ruling classes, for extending political power. Child betrothals and even infant marriage were approved for purposes of clinch-

---

[19] Will Durant, *The Story of Civilization: Part IV, The Age of Faith* (1950), p. 576.

ing property agreements. Penalties on wives for sexual infidelity originated not so much in husbandly jealousy as in the desire to protect inheritance of family property and, of course, to assuage the pride of a cuckold.

Historians are not certain how far the ladies of the manor carried their games of love beyond poetry and titillation. But the existence of the chastity belt is evidence that some feudal husbands at least had reason not to trust their wives during long absences. On the other hand, chivalric convention permitted young males open expression of passion for married women of high estate whose husbands apparently raised no objections so long as the longings and the tributes were expressed only in song or verse.

By Shakespeare's time, young love and marriage were being linked—in fiction at least. Parents still exerted their authority to choose the marital partners of their young, but public opinion in England was shifting. Some pamphleteers and poets of the period condemned parents who forced their children into wedlock out of sordid motives. A judge in the late 17th century held marriages prior to the age of seven "utterly void." A "women's lib" movement in the 18th century attacked the patriarchal system that virtually sold young women into marriage and made them the property of their husbands. Mary Wollstonecraft wrote in *Vindication of the Rights of Women,* published in 1791: "Marriage will never be held sacred till women, by being brought up with men, are prepared to be their companions rather than their mistresses."

Marriage and Divorce Laws in the United States

English settlers in America brought with them the marital customs of their group in the old country, but frontier conditions made a difference favorable to independence of the young and to raising the status of married women. The changes that took place over the years are reflected in the laws governing marriage and divorce. Marriage in New England was a civil affair; in the early years, clergymen were even forbidden to officiate at weddings. In the southern colonies, where the Church of England held sway, only the clergy were allowed to perform a valid ceremony, but the shortage of clergymen forced the extension of marrying authority to certain civil officials. In both North and South, many couples were married by unauthorized persons. Or else, if no authority was at hand, they simply lived together openly as man and wife, without social penalty. This was common-law marriage, out-

AMERICAN MARRIAGES AND DIVORCES

Year	Marriages		Divorces	
	Number (in thousands)	Rate (per 1,000 population)	Number (in thousands)	Rate (per 1,000 population)
1970 p	2,179	10.7	715	3.5
1960	1,523	8.5	393	2.2
1950	1,667	11.1	385	2.6
1940	1,595	12.1	264	2.0
1930	1,126	9.2	195	1.6
1920	1,274	12.0	170	1.6
1910	948	10.3	83	0.9
1900	709	9.3	55	0.7

p—preliminary figures.

SOURCE: NATIONAL CENTER FOR HEALTH STATISTICS.

lawed by England in 1753, but still recognized to this day by some states.

Law and custom in the United States have always favored marriage. Even today's tax law penalizes the single person. And there are other legal inducements to marry. The Rev. Robert F. Drinan, a Jesuit authority on family law and now a Democratic congressman from Massachusetts, has observed that "American law...promotes or induces marriages by means of laws designed to regulate seduction, illegitimacy, and fornication." He reported that:

• Thirty-six states make seduction a crime.

• In all states except Arizona and Oregon, some disability falls on the child born out of wedlock.

• Thirty-five states make fornication and adultery a crime, though these laws are rarely invoked.

At the same time, Father Drinan added, American law "rigorously protects the freedom of all to marry." He cited a 1965 Supreme Court decision (Griswold v. Connecticut, 381 U.S. 479) declaring unconstitutional a Connecticut law forbidding the sale or use of contraceptives. The Court "made it clear beyond question that any law restrictive of the freedom of spouses needs an uncontestable justification."[20] When the Court struck down a Virginia miscegenation law in 1967 (Loving v. Virginia, 388 U.S. 1), Chief Justice Earl Warren said "the freedom to marry has long been recognized as one of the vital personal rights essential to the orderly pursuit of happiness by free men."

---

[20] Robert F. Drinan, S.J., "American Laws Regulating the Formation of the Marriage Contract," The Annals of the American Academy of Political and Social Science, May 1969, pp. 50-53.

MEDIAN AGE OF AMERICANS AT FIRST MARRIAGE

Year	Male	Female	Year	Male	Female
1970	23.2	20.8	1930	24.3	21.3
1960	22.8	20.3	1920	24.6	21.2
1950	22.8	20.3	1910	25.1	21.6
1940	24.3	21.5	1900	25.9	21.9

Source: Census Bureau.

The only serious legal bars to marriage in the United States today are laws forbidding marriage to close relatives, age-of-consent limitations,[21] mandatory waiting periods after divorce before remarriage, and absolute strictures against polygamy. "Monogamy is so firmly rooted in American law that any exception to it or erosion of it seems unthinkable," Father Drinan wrote. On four occasions between 1878 and 1890, the Supreme Court turned down the claims of Mormons to their religious right to practice polygamy. The law's attitude toward monogamy is also reflected in the universality of adultery as a ground for divorce in state law—until recently the only ground in some states.

"Divorce by mutual consent became a sociological fact before the turn of the century, although the pretense was indulged that the law had not changed," a law professor wrote. "What had changed was the administration of the law, the appearance of the uncontested case, and the ritualization of the whole process of divorce....By the 1950s over 90 per cent of American divorces were uncontested."[22]

Divorce is indisputably popular in the United States. But so is remarriage. According to the Census Bureau, three-fourths of all divorced men and two-thirds of all divorced women remarry. One-half of the divorced men do so within two years, and one-half of the divorced women by the end of the third year.[23] Dr. Paul Glick, chief of the Population Division of the Census Bureau, said "those who remarry are much more likely to remain married until death intervenes than

---

[21] In most states parental consent for marriage is required of girls under 18 and boys under 21.

[22] Henry H. Foster Jr. (professor at New York University Law School), "The Future of Family Law." *The Annals of the American Academy of Political and Social Science,* May 1969, p. 130.

[23] U.S. Census Bureau, "Probabilities of Marriage, Divorce, and Remarriage," *Current Population Reports; Special Studies,* Series P-23, No. 32, July 29, 1970. This study is based on statistics of the period 1960-1966.

they are to become divorced." Moreover, data imply "that persons who remarry are more likely to remain in their second marriage than persons married only once are to remain in their first marriage."[24]

More than two-thirds of the adult males and nearly two-thirds of the adult females in the United States are married and living with their spouses *(see table, page 25)*. Marriage can hardly be dying out, despite reports indicating the number of single persons is growing. That growth apparently can be attributed to a rise in the average age at the time of first marriage. But though marriage remains, what is it coming to?

Visions of the Future of Marriage

THE AMERICAN MARRIAGE, Margaret Mead wrote, "is one of the most...difficult marriage forms that the human race has ever attempted."[25] For one thing, couples marry for little more reason than that they "fell in love." For another thing, they live apart from kinfolk, thus forming the so-called nuclear family. It is this family, descendant of the patriarchal family of the past, which some seers believe is due to decline—and with it the monogamous couple which forms its base.

Yet "no society anywhere has ever sanctioned illegitimacy." Anne Richardson Roiphe, who approvingly quotes those words—again Margaret Mead's—adds that "every society from aborigine to Maoist China has structured some form of family life to raise, socialize, protect the family—to guarantee institutionally the social, sexual needs of the adults." "Some of these systems have worked better than others, all of them have demanded a price from the participants—some personal freedoms and instinctual pleasures must be abandoned when human groups are formed and it is these very restrictions that enemies of the family are now calling abominations."[26]

---

[24] Quoted by Betty Rollin, "The American Way of Marriage: Remarriage," *Look*, Sept. 21, 1971, p. 62.

[25] Margaret Mead, *Male and Female* (1949), p. 342.

[26] Anne Richardson Roiphe, "The Family is Out of Fashion," *The New York Times Magazine*, Aug. 15, 1971, p. 11.

The current wave of arguments that marriage is due for a fall comes on top of an era of unprecedented effort to "make marriage work," that is, to keep marital partners happy and satisfied with each other exclusively for life. Every age has had its say about marriage, much of it in a cynical vein. But it is doubtful that any age has devoted so much attention to the problems of why married couples do not get along. Never have there been so many experts—as distinct from sages—to tell couples what to do to save their marriages.

Peculiar to this effort has been the emphasis on sexual gratification in marriage—a subject which did not much concern marital advisers of the past. This emphasis is an outgrowth of the revolt against Victorianism, which held that sexual relations were the painful duty of a wife which, if she were a good woman, she could not expect to enjoy. Post-Freudian prophets of the "new freedom" taught the post-World War I generation of youth that uninhibited sex was a sinless joy, even in marriage. Then came the marriage manuals, spelling out what to do, and how to do it, to keep marital sex exciting. As the social climate became increasingly permissive, these books and a new professional class of marriage counselor became increasingly explicit. Today's counselors advise variations of sexual behavior once considered "unnatural," if not illegal. Some now urge not only a variety of techniques but a variety of partners.

Effect of Sex-Charged Environment on Marriage

According to some critics, the emphasis on sex in marriage counseling, reinforced by the ubiquity of the sex motif in the popular media, may be toppling as many marriages as it saves. The standards of erotic performance are simply too high for the average hard-working husband and wife who cannot save all their energy for the marriage bed. Cases are told of wives whose expectations of continuing ecstasy fail to materialize and of husbands bedeviled by fear of sexual inadequacy. Monogamy may simply not be able to stand the "eroticized environment," according to Rustum and Della Roy. "The eroticization of our culture oozes from its every pore, so much so that it becomes essentially absurd to expect that all physical sexual expression for a 50-year period will be confined to the marriage partner."

From one point of view, the high incidence of divorce and the liberalization of divorce laws are indications that monogamy is no longer the proper way to describe marriage in

America. "Serial marriage," as some call it, has already produced many families with children of assorted parentage. Some consider this a good sign—a trend toward broadening human relations. J. H. Plumb, the English historian, recently commented approvingly on a household in which none of the 10 children was the offspring of both the current husband and wife. Eight were children of one parent or the other from previous marriages. The other two children were born to a former wife of the current husband while she was married to another man.

> The children, who came in all sizes and ranged from blond Nordic to jet-haired Greek, bounced around the garden, as happy as any children I have ever seen. To them, as Californians, their situation did not seem particularly odd; most of their friends had multiple parents. Indeed, to them, the odd family may have been the one that Western culture has held up as a model for two thousand years or more—the lifelong union of a man and wife...[27]

Multiple Variations Seen as Pattern of the Future

While the women's magazines and most marriage counselors continue their efforts to shore up the traditional monogamous ideal in marriage, other voices insist that times are changing and marriage must change with it. "The institution of marriage has failed to adapt itself sufficiently to current requirements," write the authors of one of the many current "marriage books." "....Marriage still is an anachronism from the days of the jungle, or at least from the days of small farms and home industries." Their recipe for overcoming the social lag is more equality between the partners, an overthrowing of vestiges of the outmoded patriarchal structure of the family handed down from the past.[28]

Others offer more drastic nostrums embodying the new ethos of sexual freedom in marriage. From sources as disparate as *The Humanist* and *Playboy* has come the argument that the only way to save monogamous marriage is by casting off some of its monogamous features. Both hold for easier divorce, because it cannot be expected that most people will remained satisfied with the same partner over a lifetime, especially now that longevity has been so far extended. Both hold that extramarital sex, when mutually condoned, can cement rather than disjoint a marriage.

---

[27] J. H. Plumb, "Odd Couples," *Horizon*, Spring 1971, p. 60.

[28] William J. Lederer and Don D. Jackson, *The Mirages of Marriage* (1968), pp. 18, 35, 37.

The *Playboy* author, Morton Hunt, concludes after reviewing sympathetically the many new variants of marital forms and non-forms: "All in all, then, the evidence is overwhelming that old-fashioned marriage is not dying and that nearly all of what passes for rebellion against it is a series of patchwork modifications enabling marriage to serve the needs of modern man without being unduly costly or painful."[29]

A marriage style that departs most from traditional monogamy—communal marriage—is already being adopted by some young people in rebellion against "the system."[30] Communal living and communal child rearing do not necessarily rule out monogamy, as witness the kibbutz system in Israel. Nearly a quarter of a century ago, B. F. Skinner, the leading voice of behavioral psychology today, pictured in *Walden II* (1948) a utopian society in which children were raised communally but marriage was monogamous.

Forty-four years ago John B. Watson, the "father" of behaviorist psychology, predicted that "in 50 years, unless there is some change, the tribal custom of marriage will no longer exist." The trend he discerned, a breakdown of family standards and a weakening of parental influence over children, has continued. While few persons today expect Watson's prediction to come true in six years, there is a growing view that in the not-so-distant future Americans will consider monogamous marriage as simply one of many options.

Feminists who look upon marriage as enslavement may choose to have children but not husbands without incurring society's disapproval. Germaine Greer may realize the dream she described in *The Female Eunuch* (1971), that of having a rural estate in Italy where children of various married and unmarried parents will grow up happily in the charge of loving caretakers and enjoy occasional visits from mothers and fathers. Others will choose to marry but will put no restrictions on the right of the partner to sexual adventures outside of marriage. Communal marriage may gain more converts. And some odd couples will stick by the old monogamous ideal "till death us do part."

---

[29] Morton Hunt, "The Future of Marriage," *Playboy*, August 1971, p. 171. *The Humanist* article was written by Rustum and Della Roy. *See footnote 1.*

[30] See "Communal Living," *E.R.R.*, 1969 Vol. II, pp. 573-594.

Status of Women

by

Helen B. Shaffer

WOMEN'S DRIVE FOR EQUAL OPPORTUNITY
Revival of Feminist Fervor Through 'Women's Lib'
New Activist Groups; Discrimination Complaints
Tightening of Federal Rules to Prevent Job Bias
Attack on Male Favoritism in Colleges, Churches
Support for Proposed 'Equal Rights' Amendment

WOMEN IN EMPLOYMENT, EDUCATION, POLITICS
Rising Proportion of Working Wives, Mothers
Women's Work: Lower Paid and Less Prestigious
Meager Female Representation in the Professions
Diminishing Number of Women in Elective Posts

ISSUES AND PORTENTS FOR EQUAL RIGHTS
Question of Feminism's Decline After Suffrage
Attempt to Link Women's Cause With Negroes'
Division Over Goals: Equal Rights or Protection
Far-Reaching Influence of New-Style Feminists

1970
Aug. 5

STATUS OF WOMEN

ANY CELEBRATION of the 50th anniversary of woman's suffrage in the United States must necessarily be tempered by the realization that the status of women in American society still has a long way to go to reach par with that of men. It was on Aug. 26, 1920, that Secretary of State Bainbridge Colby proclaimed the 19th Amendment to the Constitution granting women the right to vote. Eight days earlier, on Aug. 18, Tennessee had become the 36th state to ratify and thus validate the amendment. Postal officials will acknowledge the historic occasion by issuing on Aug. 26 a commemorative stamp in a special ceremony at Adams, Mass., birthplace of suffragist leader Susan B. Anthony.

More indicative of the anniversary mood, however, is the emergence of the women's liberation movement ("Women's Lib"), bent on finishing the job the suffragists began more than a century ago. Whether or not many women stage a strike or otherwise demonstrate for their rights on Aug. 26, as called for by Now (National Organization for Women) and endorsed by a number of other women's groups, the evidence will still point to a heightened militancy in the continuing struggle to elevate the status of women in American life.

It is a mistake to judge the strength of the new rise of feminism by the relatively small number of women who physically storm male sanctuaries or shout obscenities at male reporters. They are only the outer edge of mounting impatience among women against the secondary role which society has assigned to their sex. Like the Black Panther Party in its relationship to the Negro population, the few militant women awaken deeply buried feelings within large numbers of other women who never before consciously thought of themselves as oppressed.

Women's rights as an issue has rarely interested more than a handful of men, except as a subject for humor. Its resurgence at this time, however, may well herald a considerable change in the American life style affecting men and women alike—certainly more change than followed suffrage a half-century ago. Some observers believe the impact will be even greater than that of the black drive for status. The male editor of *The Ladies' Home Journal*, John Mack Carter, whose office was invaded March 18, 1970, by 200 feminists to voice their complaints about the contents of women's magazines, wrote later that "beneath the shrill accusations and the radical dialectic, our editors heard some convincing truths about the persistence of sexual discrimination." In an introduction to a special section of the August issue of *The Journal* which he turned over to the protesting women, Carter said: "We seemed to catch a rising note of angry self-expression among today's American women, a desire for representation, for recognition, for a broadening range of alternatives in a rapidly changing society." The new movement "may have an impact far beyond its extremist eccentricities."

Advisory boards to the federal government have taken note of the growing feminist fury. Virginia R. Allen, chairman of the President's Task Force on Women's Rights and Responsibilities, told President Nixon: "American women are increasingly aware and restive over the denial of equal opportunity, equal responsibility, equal protection of law." The Citizen's Advisory Council on the Status of Women observed that "a revival of the feminist movement has occurred during the past four years and it is greatly increasing in momentum, especially among younger women."[1]

The new awareness and restiveness of women have been heightened by social unrest and the sexual revolution. Today's feminists are a different breed from their sisters who fought for suffrage. They do not limit themselves to specific goals such as equality in employment. They are mounting an assault on an entrenched pattern of relations between the sexes that, in their eyes, demeans and restricts one-half the human race. It follows that feminist militants are in the vanguard of opposition to abortion laws which they consider a denial of a woman's control over her own body. They are for abolition of alimony for wife support if a divorcee is physically and mentally able to support herself. They are in arms against mass media presentation of women as sexual objects; some women's lib groups are calling for a boycott of products of companies that stress female sexual allure in their advertising. At the ex-

---

[1] Mrs. Allen's remarks were made public June 10, 1970, in a letter to President Nixon accompanying a task force report; the council's words are contained in *The Proposed Equal Rights Amendment to the United States Constitution: A Memorandum*, March 1970. The council was established by executive order of the President in 1963 to advise government agencies; the task force was appointed by the President in September 1969.

treme, they oppose conventional marriage in favor of "voluntary association": motherhood without a husband would become fully acceptable.[2]

New Activist Groups; Discrimination Complaints

Though only a very few women publicly protest their "second sex" status and millions of women obviously have no desire to abandon their traditional role as wife-mother-homemaker, there are signs nevertheless that pressures for equalization are moving forward. For one thing, feminine activism is bringing concrete results. Individual women, often backed by militant feminist organizations, are filing formal complaints against employers, unions, educational institutions, restaurants, and government agencies, charging discrimination against members of their sex. Three relatively new organizations have been particularly effective in bringing pressure on regulatory bodies to act on sex discrimination complaints and in initiating or supporting litigation in the field of women's rights. They are Now, founded in 1966 by Betty Friedan, author of *The Feminine Mystique*,[3] and the still newer, WEAL (Women's Equity Action League) and Human Rights for Women, Inc.

Now, based in New York, has 35 chapters around the country and claims 5,000 to 10,000 members. It appeals to discontented housewives as well as to working women and is the nearest thing to a mass organization the new feminism has produced. WEAL is made up chiefly of professional and business women and works largely in the field of legal action. Human Rights for Women, based in Washington, D.C., supplies legal aid in sex discrimination cases. These are traditionally structured organizations with specific goals to be obtained by working within the political system. In addition there are more radical groups, spawned by the New Left and the campus protest movements, which come and go under a variety of names. The best-known among them are Women's Liberation, the Radical Feminists, WITCHES (Women's International Terrorist Conspiracy from Hell) and Redstockings.

Knocking down sex barriers to men's bars may not at first sight seem a great boon to the welfare of womankind. But to the women who brought suit against McSorley's Old Ale

---

[2] See "Sexual Revolution: Myth or Reality," *E.R.R.*, 1970 Vol. I, pp. 241-257, and "Abortion Law Reform," *E.R.R.*, 1970 Vol. II, pp. 545-562.
[3] In *The Feminine Mystique* (1963), often referred to as the bible of the new feminism, Mrs. Friedan denounced the forces in society that keep women in thrall to the ideal of the sexpot and/or perfect housewife.

House in New York, the victory in court provided the satisfaction of laying down a principle. A federal judge ruled on June 25, 1970, that McSorley's, an all-male tavern since its founding in 1854, was a public place subject to the equal protection clause of the Constitution, and hence its exclusion of women customers was unconstitutional. While the ruling was on appeal to higher court, the New York City Council on July 22 enacted an ordinance to prohibit discrimination against women in bars, restaurants, and similar public places. To women of the liberation movement, segregation by sex is like segregation by race—a form of discrimination, damaging economically, socially, and psychologically. And there are many "men only" signs, seen and unseen, that block a woman's way to a good lunch—or a promotion.

Of more immediate benefit to the cause may be the feminist drive against discrimination in employment, which has begun to show results. Approximately one-fourth of the 12,000 charges of discrimination in employment brought before the Equal Employment Opportunity Commission each year involve discrimination because of sex. The commission administers Title VII of the Civil Rights Act of 1964, which forbids discrimination in employment on account of race, color, religion, national origin, or sex. Under feminist pressure, the commission toughened its stand on the employment rights of women. It voted Aug. 15, 1969, to amend its guidelines so that employers cannot be excused for practices unlawful under the federal act by claiming that those practices conform with state laws. Paradoxically, many of those state laws were enacted originally to protect women in such matters as long hours, night work and physically difficult work. The commission said such laws "have ceased to be relevant to our technology or to the expanding role of the female worker in our economy."

Federal courts in California and Oregon ruled in 1968 and 1969 that state laws protecting women workers were superseded by the sex-discrimination ban in Title VII. Attorneys General in at least six states—Michigan, North Dakota, Oklahoma, Ohio, Pennsylvania and South Dakota—and the Corporation Counsel of the District of Columbia have issued similar opinions in recent months. In several cases the employing firm has taken the initiative in suits to throw out laws limiting women's hours of work.

The U.S. Court of Appeals for the Seventh Circuit (Chicago) ruled on Sept. 26, 1969, that employers may not exclude women from jobs requiring the lifting of 35 pounds or more, but must afford each worker "a reasonable opportunity to demonstrate his or her ability to perform more strenuous jobs."[4] In a similar case the Fifth Circuit Court of Appeals (New Orleans) held that the burden of proof lies on the employer to prove he had "a factual basis for believing that... substantially all women would be unable to perform safely and efficiently the duties of the job involved."[5]

Tightening of Federal Rules to Prevent Job Bias

The Equal Employment Opportunity Commission has taken the position that employers and employment agencies cannot advertise a preference for one sex or the other unless sex is a "bona fide occupational qualification." Such jobs are said to be very few—jobs for actors and washroom attendants perhaps but not nurses or engineers or stewards of ships or planes. The commission issued a guideline on Jan. 24, 1969, holding it unlawful to place ads in "Help Wanted - Male" or "Help Wanted - Female" columns unless sex is genuinely a "bfoq." The American Newspaper Publishers Association and the Washington (D.C.) *Evening Star* have challenged this rule in a court case. Many newspapers have continued the custom of sex-separated Help Wanted columns. Only recently have individual women, moved by the new feminist fervor, begun to file charges on the want ad question.

The Supreme Court in March 1970 decided to review its first case involving a charge of sex discrimination in employment under the 1964 Civil Rights Act. At issue is the validity of a company rule that excluded a mother of young children from a position as assembly-line trainee. The Court will review an appeal from a lower federal court decision favorable to the company, Martin Marietta Corp. The case is of particular interest because G. Harrold Carswell voted with the majority of judges in appellate court who denied a petition for rehearing. When President Nixon later nominated Carswell for the Supreme Court, feminists remembered his vote and accused him of being a "sexist." Rep. Patsy T. Mink (D Hawaii) was among several women who testified against his nomination at Senate Judiciary Committee hearings. The Senate on April 8, 1970, rejected the Carswell nomination, but not on grounds of "sexism."

Complaints of violations of the Equal Pay Act of 1963 rose from 351 in 1965 to approximately 565 in fiscal 1970. Accord-

---

[4] Bowe et al *v.* Colgate Palmolive Co.
[5] Weeks *v.* Southern Bell Telephone and Telegraph Co.

ing to the Department of Labor, which administers this law, an estimated $17 million in back pay is due women workers who have been paid less than men for the same work, contrary to law. The Supreme Court laid down an important principle recently in an equal pay case involving female employees of the Wheaton Glass Co. of Millville, N.J.—that jobs need not be identical but only "substantially equal" for the equal pay rule to apply.[6] A federal district court in Dallas ruled on Oct. 8, 1969, that the traditionally all-male job of hospital orderly was substantially equal to that of the traditionally female job of nurse's aide.[7]

The Department of Justice filed suit on July 20, 1970, against Libbey-Owens-Ford, glass manufacturer, for allegedly discriminating against women in violation of the equal employment provision of the Civil Rights Act. The department asked the U.S. District Court in Toledo, Ohio, to order the company to hire, train, promote, and pay women equally with men in its five Toledo area plants. Despite this landmark action—the first time the Justice Department has gone to court to enforce the sex equality provision—women leaders are critical of alleged foot-dragging by the Nixon administration.

They were cheered on June 10, 1970, when Secretary of Labor James D. Hodgson met feminist demands by releasing guidelines for enforcing executive orders to prohibit sex discrimination by government contractors. The guidelines directed employers not to make any distinction by sex in hiring, wages, hours, or other conditions of employment; in advertising not to specify male or female help unless sex was a bona fide job requirement; not to exclude mothers of young children (unless they also excluded the fathers), not to penalize women who took time off for childbirth, and so on. But disillusionment soon set in. At the insistence of leaders of women's rights groups, Hodgson met with them on July 25 to explain his position. Saying that discrimination against women was "subtle and more pervasive" than against any other group, he added that he had "no intention of applying literally exactly the same approach for women" as for other instances of discrimination in employment. One of the women leaders, Dr. Ann Scott of

---

[6] The Supreme Court on May 18, 1970, confirmed a lower court order requiring the company to pay more than $250,000 back pay to female employees. The Court action also meant that women selector-packers would receive a 21½-cent-an-hour increase. The company had contended that male workers were worth more because they could lift and stack heavy cartons of glass containers.

[7] See Robert D. Moran's analysis, "Reducing Discrimination: Role of the Equal Pay Act," *Monthly Labor Review*, June 1970, pp. 32-33.

Williamsville, N.Y., said after the meeting: "Women have been left out again by the Nixon administration."

Women won a partial victory, however, Hodgson announced on July 31 that "goals and timetables" would be set for employment of women by federal contractors. The goals and timetables were to be determined after the government had consulted with representatives of employers, labor unions, and women's groups. A blanket application of a no-discrimination rule on all jobs was not contemplated. The sex discrimination problem differed from that of race discrimination, Hodgson said, because many women do not seek employment and many jobs sought by minority males do not attract women.

Attack on Male Favoritism in Colleges, Churches

Feminist organizations are beginning to use federal anti-discrimination laws to attack long-standing practices of sex discrimination in higher education. The prevalence of government contract work in universities gives the militants a handle for bringing pressure. Favoritism toward males in hiring faculty members and admitting students to graduate and professional schools henceforth might mean the loss of a government contract. Two of the new women's organizations, Now and WEAL, have taken the lead here. They have named at least 100 colleges and universities in making complaints to federal agencies that administer the university contracts. The *Chronicle of Higher Education* reported in its issue of June 1, 1970, that government investigators had gone to Harvard and several other campuses. Some institutions—the University of Chicago is one—have responded to rising feminist pressure by setting up investigating committees of their own.

Not all of the push is coming from new militant groups. The 88-year-old American Association of University Women has brought a complaint against the U.S. Office of Education for failing—despite frequent pleas—to show sex differentials in faculty rank and pay when collecting and analyzing data in higher education. The need is great for "objective data to support what we know is flagrant discrimination against women in academia," AAUW representative Ruth M. Oltman told *Editorial Research Reports*. The President's task force had made a similar recommendation. In the course of a recent survey, the association itself uncovered several hundred case histories of sex discrimination in higher education and hundreds more of job discrimination against educated women.

Women are ignoring St. Paul's admonition that they "keep silence in the churches." They are demanding—and to some degree, getting—their "rights" in leading American religious groups. Women delegates warned the American Baptist Convention in May 1970 that they would demand a woman be named president at the following year's meeting. The National Council of Churches in December 1969 chose its first woman president, Cynthia Wedel. The Lutheran Church in America yielded to feminist pressure by changing its bylaws on June 29, 1970, to permit women to become ordained ministers. Approximately one-fourth of the 235 member churches of the World Council of Churches ordain women. Some orders of Roman Catholic nuns have adopted secular practices to avoid submission to the church's "male mystique."[8] Perhaps most extraordinary of all, a girl is studying to become a rabbi at a Hebrew seminary in Cincinnati.

Support for Proposed 'Equal Rights' Amendment

Another sign of the new wave of feminist militancy is the revival of support for an "Equal Rights" amendment to the Constitution. The proposed amendment, stating simply that "Equality of rights under the law shall not be denied or abridged by the United States or by any state on account of sex," has been introduced in every session of Congress since 1923. Backers of the amendment have never been able to win congressional approval so that it could be presented to the various state legislatures for ratification.

But in 1970 there was a new basis for hope. Rep. Martha W. Griffiths (D Mich.) extricated the proposal from the House Judiciary Committee, a burial ground for the measure in years past, by getting the required 218 signatures of members on a discharge petition. Once this was done the measure was scheduled for floor action, expected about Aug. 10. In the Senate, the proposal received its first hearings in 14 years and afterward won approval of the Constitutional Amendments Subcommittee. The subcommittee chairman, Birch Bayh (D Ind.), one of 82 senators sponsoring the proposal, predicted approval by the parent Senate Judiciary Committee and then floor action later in the session.

At least a dozen bills pending in Congress in August 1970 were aimed specifically at removing some form of discrimination against women. Rep. Edith Green (D Ore.) introduced a measure to (1) prohibit sex discrimination in any program

---

[8] See Joseph H. Fichter, "Holy Father Church," *Commonweal*, May 15, 1970, p. 216.

receiving federal financial assistance, (2) extend coverage of the Equal Pay Act of 1963 to executive, administrative and professional employees, and (3) extend the jurisdiction of the Civil Rights Commission to include cases of sex discrimination. Hearings on her proposals were held June 16-19. Another measure would, if passed, strengthen the enforcement powers of the Equal Employment Opportunity Commission, and extend coverage of the Civil Rights Act to include sex discrimination in academic and professional employment. Other measures would remedy inequities that working wives suffer under the Social Security Act, provide day care facilities for children of working women, and equalize treatment of married women and married men in the federal service in regard to housing and other benefits overseas and to survivorship benefits. These proposals for legislation also follow recommendations of the President's Task Force on the Rights and Responsibilities of Women.

All told, the women's rights movement appears to be moving ahead, especially on the job front. Sonia Pressman, a senior lawyer for the Equal Employment Opportunity Commission, told a meeting of labor relations officials in Boston, April 29, 1970: "What we have seen in the past five years is nothing short of a revolution—a revolution in the legal rights of women to equality on the job and a revolution in the expectations of women with regard to such equality." However, she added: "There has not yet been a corresponding revolution in the employment status of women—in the jobs they hold and the salaries they earn."

Women in Employment, Education, Politics

THE STRONGEST drive for sex equality comes from working women. Entry into the labor force puts a hard dollars-and-cents value on equal rights. This is true of nearly all women who work, whether in factories, in offices, or in the professions. The continuing growth of the female labor force, especially the recent spurt upward, has therefore been a great stimulus to the women's rights movement. Nearly 31 million American women worked in early 1970, accounting for two-fifths of the entire labor force. Working women composed 42 per cent of all women 16 or older, in contrast to 23 per cent (8.2 million) half a century earlier.

51

Equally significant is the rising percentage of wives and mothers who work. The typical working woman in 1920 was single; if she married she quit work for good unless widowhood or desertion left her with no other means of support. The current pattern for a woman who marries is to remain employed, quitting only a few years for child-bearing and child-rearing. Two-fifths of all married women are in the labor force today compared with one-fourth in the mid-1950s. Wives accounted for 30 per cent of all working women in 1949 but 60 per cent in 1970.[9] An acceleration of the working-wife trend in recent years is due largely to younger women. The portion of wives under 35 in the labor market rose from 28 to 40 per cent during the past decade, with the steepest increases occurring in 1968-69.[10] One-third of all women with children of pre-school age were working or seeking work in 1969, almost twice as many as nine years earlier. Among mothers whose children had reached school age, almost one-half were working.

Although feminism is strongest among working women, the much-reported discontent among young housewives adds another spur to the equalization movement. This discontent is manifested mainly among college-educated young women who find routine homemaking tasks dull and damaging to the image of themselves acquired during their college days. The relatively high level of female education in the United States thus contributes to the many forces pressing on women to seek a fuller life beyond the sphere of domesticity.

The great growth in higher education of women occurred during the early decades of this century. The proportion of women earning college degrees fell during the 1940s, to pick up sharply in the 1950s for bachelor degrees but much more slowly for advanced degrees. As of March 1968 some 4.5 million women above age 25 had completed at least four years of college. The figure was sure to grow rapidly. Another study showed that one-fifth of all 21-year-old women were college graduates.[11]

---

[9] Elizabeth Waldman, "Changes in the Labor Force Activities of Women," *Monthly Labor Review*, June 1970, p. 11. A higher portion of Negro wives work than white wives but the gap is narrowing. As of March 1969, 51 per cent of Negro wives and 39 per cent of white wives were in the labor force.

[10] In the 12-month period that ended in March 1969, the total working population grew by 1.8 million and working wives accounted for 43 per cent of that increase. Among these 775,000 wives, 300,000 were ages 20-24. The baby boom after World War II only partly explains why women in this age group are so numerous in the work force. Their portion of the population rose by one-third between 1960 and 1969 but their participation in the labor force more than doubled.

[11] Department of Labor, *Trends in Educational Attainment of Women*, October 1969, pp. 5, 12.

The more education a woman has, the more likely she is to be engaged in paid employment, regardless of her marital status. The following table shows the relationship:

Education	Employed
5 years college or more	71 per cent
4 years college	54 per cent
High school graduation	48 per cent
Less than 8 years schooling	24 per cent

A Department of Labor study for the years 1952-68 showed exceptionally high employment for highly educated women in the 20-24 and 45-54 age groups. Particularly significant, however, was that among women college graduates the greatest increase in labor force participation came from the 25-34 age group. This is normally a period when women shun outside jobs because of small children in the family.

Women's Work: Lower Paid and Less Prestigious

Labor force participation does not tell the whole story of woman's status in employment. Though most of the legal barriers to equality of opportunity in the work world have fallen away, the over-all picture for the woman worker has not changed very much in the half-century since women got the vote. Women still get the poorest paying, least prestigious jobs;[12] they are still scarce in the professions except for traditional and relatively low-paid careers in nursing, school teaching, and social work; and they have not captured more than a handful of commanding positions in business, education or other fields. Moreover, women workers are unemployed more often than men.[13]

Male-female pay differences run down the occupational scales from top to bottom, just as they did a half-century ago. On a percentage basis, women's pay has fallen further behind men's in recent years, as the following Department of Labor statistics illustrate.

Year	Women	Men	Salary income as % of men's
1955	$2,719	$4,252	63.9
1960	3,293	5,417	60.8
1965	3,823	6,375	60.0
1968	4,457	7,664	58.2

[12] "No matter what sphere of work women are hired for or select, like sediment in a wine bottle they seem to settle to the bottom."—Cynthia Fuchs Epstein, *Woman's Place* (1970), p. 2. See "Women's Place in the Economy," *E.R.R.*, 1957 Vol. I, p. 8.

[13] Unemployment rates in 1969 averaged 2.8 per cent for men and 4.9 per cent for women. Unemployment rates for white women were more favorable, however, than for non-white men. Figures for 1969 were 2.5 per cent for white males; 3.8 per cent for white females; 4.3 per cent for non-white males and 5.8 per cent for non-white females.

The pay gap varies by occupation. But even where it is smallest, in the professional-technical worker and clerical worker categories, a woman's earnings are only about two-thirds as high as a man's. Among other workers the gap widens, to the point that women sales workers earn less than one-half what their male counterparts do. (See table, opposite page.) Another measure of the gap in the earnings of women and men who work full-time the year-round is shown in the following table of wage-salary income distribution for the year 1968.

Earnings	Women	Men	Earnings	Women	Men
	(in percentages)			*(in percentages)*	
Less than $3,000	20.0	7.5	$7,000 to $10,000	10.9	30.9
$3,000 to $5,000	40.0	12.6	$10,000 to $15,000	2.5	19.5
$5,000 to $7,000	26.0	23.1	$15,000 and over	0.4	8.2

There is no indication that the trend has been reversed since 1968 when the foregoing statistics were gathered. A study of expected salaries for June 1970 college graduates indicated that women entering upon careers in accounting, chemistry, economics, engineering, liberal arts and mathematics could expect to earn anywhere from $86 to $18 less per month than male graduates.[14] The inability of women to move up the managerial and professional ladders, even when they are qualified to do so, accounts in part for their relatively low pay. The Equal Employment Opportunity Commission released statistics in 1969 indicating that women and non-white males were often engaged in work far below their abilities and educational qualifications. Another survey involving 150 business companies showed that only one in ten had as many as 5 per cent of its managerial positions filled with women. Four companies in ten had no women in the higher ranks of management.[15]

Meager Female Representation in the Professions

American women comprise only seven per cent of the nation's physicians,[16] four per cent of its architects, three per

---

[14] Frank S. Endicott, *Trends in Employment and University Graduates in Business and in Industry* (publication of Northeastern University, 1970).

[15] American Society for Personnel Administration-Bureau of National Affairs, *ASPA-BNA Survey: Employment of Women* (1970).

[16] Of 29 countries reporting to the Medical Women's International Association recently, the United States ranked 26th in the percentage of doctors who are women. Only Madagascar, Spain and South Viet Nam ranked lower. Women comprised 25 per cent of the doctors in Finland, Israel, and the Philippines; 20 per cent in Germany, 16 per cent in England, 13 per cent in France.

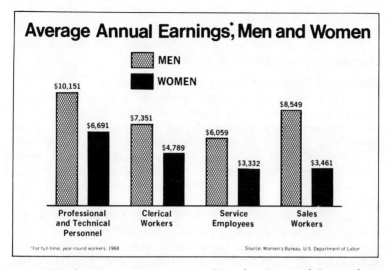

Average Annual Earnings, Men and Women

- ▨ MEN
- ■ WOMEN

$10,151 · $6,691 · $7,351 · $4,789 · $8,549 · $6,059 · $3,332 · $3,461

| Professional and Technical Personnel | Clerical Workers | Service Employees | Sales Workers |

*For full-time, year-round workers, 1968

Source: Women's Bureau, U.S. Department of Labor

cent of its lawyers, two per cent of its dentists and fewer than one per cent of its engineers. Even in professions in which women predominate, they rarely rise to the top. Seventy per cent of all teachers are women but the higher one goes on the educational and pay scales, the scarcer women become. Only one-fifth of all college teachers are women and few of them are in prestigious institutions or hold high-ranking professorial posts.[17] Even in areas of education where women predominate, men are often found in top positions. Males often head women's colleges.[18] Nine out of ten elementary school teachers are women but only about two of every ten principals are women.[19]

Perhaps the greatest disappointment of the women's rights movement is that so few women have held public office. Mrs. Carrie Chapman Catt had warned her fellow suffragists on the eve of victory that winning the vote would not admit them to the inner sanctum of political power; a "locked door" would still bar their entry. "You will have a long hard fight before you get behind that door," she said, "...but if you really

---

[17] The University of Chicago faculty, in the spring of 1969, included only 81 women among its 1,179 members. Only 11 of 476 full professors were women. These ratios "compare favorably...with those universities which...view themselves as 'elite'."—University of Chicago Committee on Women.

[18] Men hold presidencies of Bryn Mawr, Mount Holyoke, Sarah Lawrence and Vassar. A tendency to appoint men presidents of prestigious women's colleges may be related to moves to convert them to co-educational institutions.

[19] Report on sampling of 365 members of the National Education Association's Department of Elementary School Principals, *The National Elementary Principal*, November 1969, p. 81. See also Department of Labor, *1969 Handbook on Women Workers*, p. 97.

want women's vote to count, make your way there."[20] Few
women have made it behind that locked door; in partisan
politics, the pattern of male chairman and female vice-
chairman prevails almost universally.[21]

Diminishing Number of Women in Elective Posts

As for winning elective office, women have actually back-
slid. Only 11 women—six Democrats and five Republicans—
were among the 535 members of Congress in 1970, eight
fewer than in 1961-62 when their numbers reached an all-
time high of 19. In the entire 54-year period since Rep. Jeannette Rankin (R Mont.) became the first woman to be elected
to Congress [22] in 1916, only 75 women have served in the
federal legislature. Only 10 of them have been senators. One
of these, Sen. Margaret Chase Smith (R Maine), now in her
fourth term, is unique for having made political office a lifetime career and having attained recognition as one of the
more able and influential members of the Senate.[23] Her
nearest rival in effectiveness, Mrs. Maurine B. Neuberger (D
Ore.), was elected to the Senate in 1960 after having served
three terms in the state legislature. She did not stand for re-
election in 1966. The route to the Senate for all 10 led through
widowhood, each having been appointed or elected to fill the
term of a deceased husband. Seven of the ten served only a
few months or less. Sen. Hattie Caraway (D Ark.), appointed
in 1931 and re-elected until defeated in 1944, was a passive
figure in the Senate, though through seniority she became
chairman of a minor committee.[24]

Among the 66 women who have served in the House of Representatives, only a few have wielded significant power in that
body. Prominent among them were Edith Nourse Rogers (R

---

[20] Address before League of Women Voters' first congress, Chicago, Feb. 14, 1920,
cited by Eleanor Flexner, *Century of Struggle: The Woman's Rights Movement in the
United States* (1959), p. 326.

[21] Edward J. Flynn, former Democratic National Chairman, described the ideal national committeewoman: "She must be handsome, a lady, able to introduce the President gracefully, and wear orchids well; she must have an acceptable bank account—and
she must never, never interfere with party policy."—Quoted by Barbara Wendell Kerr,
"Don't Kid the Women," *Woman's Home Companion*, October 1956, p. 4.

[22] Miss Rankin served two widely separated single terms—in 1917-18 and again in
1941-42. In each term she cast a lonely vote against a declaration of war. In recent
years Miss Rankin has given public support to women's peace movements. See CQ
Weekly Report, July 10, 1970, pp. 1745-1748.

[23] Mrs. Smith was a member of the Republican State Committee in Maine (1930-
36), secretary to Rep. Clyde H. Smith (R Maine) whom she married, congresswoman
1940-48, and senator, 1949 to the present.

[24] Mrs. Caraway "seldom spoke on the Senate floor, preferring to do crossword
puzzles during debate....[She] frequently made the statement that she always voted the
way 'Thad' [her deceased husband, Sen. Thaddeus Caraway] would have voted."—
Martin Gruber, *Women in American Politics: An Assessment and Sourcebook* (1968),
p. 124.

WOMEN MEMBERS OF CONGRESS

Years	Senate	House	Years	Senate	House
1947-48	0	8	1959-60	1	16
1949-50	1	9	1961-62	2	17
1951-52	1	10	1963-64	2	11
1953-54	2	11	1965-66	2	10
1955-56	1	16	1967-68	1	11
1957-58	1	15	1969-70	1	10

Mass.), who served 18 terms (1925-60), Mary T. Norton (D N.J.), 13 terms (1925-50), and Frances Payne Bolton (R Ohio), 14 terms (1941-68). The 10 congresswomen now in office are highly regarded as effective and independent-minded legislators. Most of them have displayed strong staying powers. The only first-termer is the first Negro woman to serve in Congress, Shirley Chisholm of Brooklyn, who has said "in the political world I have been far oftener discriminated against because I am a woman than because I am black."[25]

The women's division of the Republican National Committee counted 306 women of both major parties serving in state legislatures in 1970, about 40 fewer than 10 years earlier. The 306 are spread over the legislatures of 49 states; only New Hampshire has a sizable number (62). Larger urbanized states, particularly, have few women legislators. New York has four, California three and New Jersey one.

The prospect of a woman President is as remote as ever[26] and that of a woman governor serving in her own right almost as inconceivable. Of the three women who actually have been elected governor, all served as shadows of their husbands. Nellie Tayloe Ross, a Democrat, was elected governor of Wyoming in 1924 to fill out two years of her deceased husband's term but was defeated in 1926 for re-election. James E. Ferguson, who had been impeached and removed as governor of Texas in 1917, successfully campaigned in 1924 for the election of his wife, using the slogan "Two governors for the price of one." Mrs. Miriam A. ("Ma") Ferguson was defeated in 1928, but re-elected in 1932, with her husband again serving as mentor. Lurleen Wallace was elected governor of

[25] See *CQ Weekly Report*, July 10, 1970, pp. 1745-48. Other congresswomen today are Leonor K. Sullivan (D Mo.), Edith Green (D Ore.), Martha W. Griffiths (D Mich.), Florence P. Dwyer (R N.J.), Julia B. Hansen (D Wash.), Catherine May (R Wash.), Patsy T. Mink (D Hawaii), Charlotte T. Reid (R Ill.), and Margaret M. Heckler (R Mass.).

[26] Three women received one or more votes for the presidential nomination at the 1924 Democratic convention. Nellie Tayloe Ross received 31 votes on the first ballot in 1928 for the Democratic vice-presidential nomination. Sen. Margaret Chase Smith received 30 votes in 1964 for the Republican presidential nomination.

Alabama in 1966 as a sit-in for her husband, George A. Wallace, who was constitutionally barred from succeeding himself.[27]

Only 31 women hold state elective positions outside the legislatures, a drop from 41 a decade earlier. Five are secretaries of state, 11 are state treasurers, two are state supreme court justices.[28] The meager showing in elective office is matched by lists of women appointees. In its publication *Women in Public Service*, the Republican National Committee listed 309 women appointed to "key positions in the federal government, in international affairs, and on important committees and commissions" in the first 16 months of the Nixon administration. Thirty-five of the posts were described as "high-level, policy-making positions." These positions, however, tended to be concerned with what are regarded as traditional women's interests. Another list of 273 women in federal service, offered as a sampling of "the type of positions women have achieved," included two ambassadors (Carol Laise to Nepal and Eileen R. Donovan to Barbados), an Assistant Secretary of Health, Education and Welfare (Patricia Hitt) and six members of U.S. missions to the United Nations.

Women's organizations long have pushed for more appointments of women to governmental posts. The National Federation of Business and Professional Women's Clubs maintains a "talent bank"—a roster of names and biographies of exceptionally qualified women—which it regularly submits to the White House. The federation and other organizations concerned with women's status are particularly concerned that there is no woman member of the President's cabinet and that no woman has ever been appointed to the Supreme Court.[29]

Male prejudice against women in high office, usually kept politely under cover, came to the surface when Rep. Patsy T. Mink (D Hawaii), at a meeting of the Democrats' Committee on National Priorities, April 30, 1970, urged that women's

---

[27] Mrs. Wallace died in office in May 1968. Wallace, now seeking re-election himself, won the Democratic nomination in June 1970 and is without a Republican opponent in November.

[28] The states with women in these elective offices are Alabama, Arkansas, Arizona, California, Colorado, Connecticut, Idaho, Kansas, Kentucky, Louisiana, Mississippi, New Mexico, North Dakota, North Carolina, Pennsylvania, South Dakota and Wyoming.

[29] The only two women cabinet officers were Secretary of Labor Frances Perkins in the Franklin D. Roosevelt administration, and Secretary of Health, Education and Welfare Oveta Culp Hobby in the Eisenhower administration. Eight women today are judges of federal courts. Of the nation's entire roster of 8,750 judges, 300 are women, most of whom serve on county courts.

rights be given high priority. Mrs. Mink was challenged by a member of the committee, Dr. Edgar F. Berman, an ex-surgeon and close friend of former Vice President Hubert H. Humphrey. Dr. Berman contended that women were disqualified for jobs requiring important decisions because their menstrual cycle and menopause subjected them to "raging hormonal influences." A furor ensued when his remarks were divulged publicly some three months later and he was prompted to resign from the committee.

Issues and Portents for Equal Rights

FEMINIST LEADERS ponder today why feminism failed. Some say it is because women relaxed once they got the vote. Others say it is because the feminist movement became too narrowly concentrated on suffrage and lost connection with its revolutionary origins. "In many ways [the suffrage movement] was the red herring of the revolution—a wasteful drain on the energy of 70 years," writes Kate Millett, leading theorist of the women's lib. "Because the opposition was so monolithic and unrelenting, the struggle so long and bitter, the vote took on a disproportionate importance. And when the ballot was won, the feminist movement collapsed."[30] Women divided their support between the two major parties pretty much as men did. Some did not even bother to vote and women candidates could not count on the support of those who did. Once suffrage was won, no feminist issue carried much political weight.

The situation is not entirely different now. The percentage of women who vote has increased until it has nearly reached that of men.[31] Because of the higher portion of women in the voter-age population (53.3 per cent), women voters in 1968 actually outnumbered men (40 million to 38 million). Yet feminism is not a major political issue, though some persons in the women's rights movement predict that it will enter into the 1972 election.

---

[30] Kate Millett, *Sexual Politics* (1970), p. 83.

[31] In 1924, only one-third of the women but two-thirds of the men voted in national elections. In November 1968, 66 per cent of the women and 69.8 per cent of the men voted —U.S. Census Bureau, "Voting and Registration in the Election of November 1968" (Population Characteristics, Series P-20), pp. 10-11.

The battle to win the vote had been a heroic one. Over the half-century between the first introduction of the suffrage amendment in Congress in 1866 and final victory, the suffragists had conducted 480 campaigns to get legislatures to submit suffrage amendments to voters; 47 campaigns to get state constitutional conventions to write woman's suffrage into state constitutions; 277 campaigns to get state party conventions to include woman's suffrage planks; 30 campaigns to get national party conventions to adopt woman's suffrage planks in party platforms; and 19 campaigns with 19 successive Congresses.[32]

Suffragists suffered pain, contumely and arrest; they were the butt of jokes and insults. The unattractive image of the battle-axe feminist, devoid of feminine charm, rejected by men, and even a bit off her rocker—an image created by publicists for the opposition—is a heritage which still taints the feminist movement and makes many secretly sympathetic women leery of the label. Prominent among the anti-suffrage interests was the liquor industry, which had reason to fear women prohibitionists in the era of the corner saloon.[33]

In the end the doughty crusaders had no effective program for women's rights beyond suffrage. This was not true in the beginning. Pioneer feminists of the early 19th century had begun what then seemed an almost hopeless battle against an entrenched way of life, solidified by law, moral conviction, and religion, which kept women and especially married women in the status of chattels or at best dependent children. The early movement was by no means confined to a struggle for suffrage. More immediate concerns were control of property, of earnings, guardianship, divorce, opportunity for education and employment, lack of legal status, and the concept of female inferiority perpetuated by established religion.

The Woman's Rights Convention at Seneca Falls, N.Y., in July 1848 is generally cited as the beginning of the woman's suffrage movement in the United States. But the Declaration of Principles which Mrs. Elizabeth Cady Stanton read at that meeting and which thereafter became a sacred text of the movement, was a much broader and more revolutionary document than a simple claim for the franchise. Paraphrasing the

---

[32] Carrie Chapman Catt's tally, cited by Eleanor Flexner, *Century of Struggle: The Woman's Rights Movement in the United States* (1969), p. 173.

[33] Suffrage has been unfairly blamed for prohibition, however. Women had not received the vote nationwide when the 18th Amendment (prohibition) became effective in early 1920. At that time they could cast a ballot only in the individual states that had already granted them the franchise.

Declaration of Independence, it held "these truths to be self-evident: that all men and women are created equal." It itemized woman's grievances—"a history of repeated injuries and ursurpations on the part of man toward woman"—and pledged an unremitting fight, in the face of anticipated punishment from society, to attain the goal of equality. The meeting adopted a number of resolutions, unanimously except for one —a call for woman suffrage, which carried by a small margin.

Attempt to Link Women's Cause With Negroes'

Today's new breed of feminists tends to equate the role of women with that of the black—an analogy irritating to many blacks—and to link their cause with that of the racial minorities as a struggle against the dominance of the white man in American society. The linkage has a historical precedent in the close association of women's rights and the anti-slavery movement beginning in the 1830s. "The first conscious feminists," Eleanor Flexner wrote, were women who learned in the fight to free the slaves how to fight for their own rights.

> It was in the abolition movement that women first learned to organize, to hold public meetings, to conduct petition campaigns. As abolitionists they first won the right to speak in public and began to evolve a philosophy of their place in society and of their basic rights. For a quarter of a century the two movements, to free the slave and liberate the woman, nourished and strengthened one another.

It was the sharpest of disappointments that the 14th Amendment—and then the 15th—failed to include women in the extension of citizenship rights to Negroes. "Many of the early suffragists never recovered from their humiliating discovery that Negro men were considered better qualified to vote than they. In consequence, it became customary for them to exploit racial prejudices to their own advantage."[34]

The suffrage cause became more and more marked by the prejudices of upper-middle-class women in the post-Civil War period. Negro women were segregated or discouraged from joining suffrage parades. Rather than argue against the degradation and exploitation of women, the suffragists offered woman suffrage as a means of putting down blacks and the foreign-born. In effect, they appealed for a restricted franchise that would give middle-class women the vote but deny it to the despised classes. Though the suffrage movement dropped this bid for support in the last decade of the struggle, it left

---

[34] William L. O'Neill, *Everyone Was Brave: The Rise and Fall of Feminism in America* (1969), p. 69.

among working women a residue of hostility toward the women's rights movement.

Division Over Goals: Equal Rights or Protection

This division was most concretely expressed in the post-suffrage debate over the proposed Equal Rights amendment. Women's organizations for years were sharply divided on the amendment. The National Woman's Party has been almost solely concerned with its adoption but the party has never had much rank-and-file appeal. The amendment's chief supporters over the years have been business and professional women, represented by the National Federation of Business and Professional Women's Clubs. On the other side were women in trade unions and in social reform organizations who believed it would be detrimental to the majority of working women and would throw out laws protecting married women and children. They fought instead for the array of social reform legislation—wage-hour laws, child labor bans, social security and welfare measures, provisions for maternal-child health and other public health programs.

On the question of equal rights, they have held that men and women should be treated equitably but not necessarily identically where their interests differ. The success in putting over this point of view in the post-suffrage years is indicated by the vast body of legislation and regulation protective of women—limiting hours, forbidding night work, setting minimum wages in low-paid, woman-dominated employment, and so forth. Only in recent years has support for this body of law, now falling away under the hammer of the Civil Rights Act, been declining. Two formidable organizations, the League of Women Voters and the American Association of University Women, dropped their opposition to the Equal Rights amendment some years ago.

The strongest opponent today is organized labor, a frequent target of feminists who regard it as just another male-dominated institution controlling the lives of women. Women compose 20 per cent of the total membership of labor unions but occupy virtually none of the leadership positions. Even unions with large female memberships, like those in the clothing trades, have always been headed by men.

A new breed of feminists is determined to give up the privileges as well as the penalties of lower-level status. It is in keeping with the current mood that the latest of a series of presidential study groups on the question of women's rights—

each President in recent years having felt the need to appease women with such a study—emphasizes "responsibilities" as well as the "rights" of women. The return to radical feminism is by no means confined to women of the guerrilla theater stamp. The vision of the "new woman" pressed by radical feminists has come within view of old-line women's organizations. An infusion of activist energy from black women and young women fresh off the campus has reached these relatively conservative strongholds of feminist power.

Dividing lines between the old and new brands of feminism may be disappearing. Mrs. Elizabeth Duncan Koontz, director of the Women's Bureau in the Department of Labor, has belittled the theory that the sexes have to be "highly distinct in their roles, polarized in their interests and abilities." She joined the new feminists in criticizing the education system, the news media, the advertising trade, and child-rearing dicta as conditioning women to accept a second-rung status, limited in range of activity. The influence of new feminism has also reached the Young Women's Christian Association, which issued a *Work Book* at its 1970 convention in Houston stating: "It is essential that women move beyond being sexual playthings of the male to an affirmation of their role as human beings, with capacity for leadership and contribution in varied ways....They need an identity of their own."

What this closing of the ranks will mean to the future status of women is not certain. The great majority of women give little evidence that they object to the status quo. The chief determinant of the future may be simply the need of the economy—and the individual family—for the earnings of the wife-and-mother. In the end it may be that the husband and wife will routinely share in both housework and family earnings. Now has proposed paternity as well as maternity leave for employees so that mothers can pursue careers and fathers can have more time with the children. Some men may even get to like it that way.

CHILD CARE

by

Mary Costello

CHILD CARE AND NATIONAL POLITICS
Increase in Working Mothers and Day-Care Needs
Question of Federal Responsibility for Children
Extent and Cost of Services Currently Available
Passage and Veto of Mondale Plan for Full Care

SPORADIC GROWTH OF CHILD SERVICES
Founding of Private Day Nurseries in 19th Century
Child-Study Centers and WPA Pre-School Projects
Centers for Workers' Children in World War II
Popularity of Head Start; Questioning of Benefits

PROBLEMS AND PROSPECTS FOR CHILD CARE
Arrangements and Facilities in Foreign Countries
Demands From Movement for Women's Equality
Effect of Group Care on Children Under Three
Financial Drawbacks to the Expansion of Day Care

1 9 7 2
June 14

CHILD CARE

DAY CARE FOR CHILDREN, a social issue already thrust into the political arena, is destined to become increasingly important in the years ahead. Enthusiasts see it as a way of reducing welfare costs, giving many young children opportunities they would not have otherwise for mental, physical and emotional development, and allowing women from all income levels to seek work outside the home. Opponents argue that day care promotes a communal rather than a family approach to child rearing, that it can be psychologically harmful, especially to very young children, that it encourages more women to enter an already crowded labor force, and finally that the cost of providing quality day-care services to all who want or even need them would be prohibitive.

One fact stands out amid the arguments: the number of child-care facilities is inadequate for the growing demand. The Office of Child Development in the Department of Health, Education and Welfare (HEW) reports that there are more than five million children of pre-school age whose mothers work. The total capacity of licensed public and private day-care facilities is less than 700,000. This means that the vast majority of working mothers must make other arrangements for the care of their children when they are on the job.

Government-sponsored studies have revealed that almost half of the under-six children were cared for at home *(see table, p. 69)*—by fathers who often worked night shifts and spent much of the day sleeping, by older children and untrained babysitters. Others went with their mothers to work and amused themselves as best they could. Still others were left with neighbors or relatives where the only stimulation might be the television set. Most disturbing of all, thousands of pre-school children fended for themselves without any adult supervision.

Children of mothers now working are not the only potential users of day-care facilities. There are more than 2.5 million pre-schoolers whose families are below the poverty line and whose mothers are not employed. Labor Department studies have shown that many of these women wanted to work but were unable to find care for their children. Families just above the poverty line, the "near poor" who have yearly incomes of $4,000 to $8,000, do not qualify for federally assisted day care and frequently cannot afford any other. In addition, many of the 33 million children between the ages of six and 13 need some adult supervision from the time school is dismissed until their parents return from work.

"The number of children of working mothers in need of care has been rising considerably more rapidly than the supply of services available," the National Council of Jewish Women reported in early 1972 after conducting a two-year survey. "In community after community, the people most knowledgeable about day-care needs and existing services told council interviewers that an eight or ten fold or greater expansion of day care would not suffice."[1] Behind the growing demand is a far-reaching change taking place in American family life. Since 1950 the percentage of mothers who work has almost doubled *(see table, p. 82)*.

Separated, widowed and divorced women bringing up children on their own have always worked in large numbers. But the increase in recent years is not primarily the result of family breakups. It is identified largely with changing attitudes toward the "woman's place" in society—change that is pushed by the movement for women's equality and perhaps accelerated by a trend toward small families, urban living, and high education levels. The chances are greater that a mother will be working if she is well educated, lives in a metropolitan area, has few children, and believes her family needs the money.

Questions of Federal Responsibility for Children

In vetoing a bill to expand the government's role in child care *(see p. 73)*, President Nixon declared that "such far-reaching national legislation should not, must not, be enacted in the absence of a great national debate upon its merits and broad public acceptance of its principles." The Brookings Institution in Washington, D.C., addressed itself to this question in a study of federal budget priorities.[2] The Brookings authors, including Charles L. Schultze, a former budget director, found the possibilities for child care include

---

[1] Mary Dublin Keyserling, *Windows on Day Care* (a report on the findings of the National Council of Jewish Women, 1972).

[2] Charles L. Schultze and others, "Child Care," *Setting National Priorities: The 1973 Federal Budget* (1972), pp. 252-290.

CHILD-CARE ARRANGEMENTS OF WORKING MOTHERS

Arrangement	Children under age 6		Children ages 6-14	
	1965	1970	1965	1970
Care in own home	48.0%	49.9%	66.0%	78.7%
By father	14.4	18.8	15.1	10.6
By other relative	17.5	18.9	22.6	20.6
By a nonrelative	15.3	7.3	6.8	4.5
Mother worked only during school hours	0.8	5.2	21.5	42.9
Care in some other home	30.7	34.5	9.2	12.6
By a relative	14.9	15.5	4.7	7.6
By a nonrelative	15.8	19.0	4.5	5.0
Day-care center	5.6	10.5	0.6	0.6
No special care	15.7	5.0	24.3	8.3
Totals*	100.0	100.0	100.0	100.0

*Figures may not add to totals because of rounding.
SOURCES: Brookings Institution, based on data from the U.S. Women's Bureau, U.S. Children's Bureau, Office of Economic Opportunity

---

custodial, aimed primarily at keeping the children from harm; *developmental*, focusing on pre-school education, nutrition and health needs; and *comprehensive*, which includes the foregoing plus parent education in nutrition, health and child development.

Aside from these choices, there are questions as to whether the government should finance and even operate the programs or confine itself to setting standards. If there is financing, should it be indirect (giving a subsidy to parents through vouchers or tax relief), or direct? And should the programs be open to everyone or limited to the needy? If the latter course is chosen, there is the problem of defining who is "needy."

Decisions about day care and early childhood programs are likely to provoke a heated national debate over the next few years [the Brookings authors wrote], not only because the budgetary consequences might be large, but because sensitive emotional issues are involved. How should the responsibility for children be divided between the family and society? Should mothers of small children work? The spectrum of views is wide....

Traditionally in the United States, the responsibility for the care and supervision of children has rested squarely with parents. Only when a child reached age six did society at large take a major hand by insisting that he attend school.... What happens to the child the rest of the time is his parents' business. Society intervenes only if he is severely abused or neglected or runs afoul of the law.

FEDERAL SPENDING FOR CHILD-CARE PROGRAMS

(in millions of dollars)

Program	1970	1971	1972*	1973*
Day care	164	233	404	507
Head Start	330	363	364	369
Pre-school programs under Elementary and Secondary Education Act, Title 1	26	92	98	93
Total	520	688	866	969

*Estimates

SOURCES: Senate Finance Committee, Office of Budget and Management

---

It is pointed out that many communities provide free kindergarten for five-year-olds but few offer nursery care for younger children. Some health services are available for children but nothing so comprehensive as Medicare for the aged. And welfare programs have traditionally been designed to reduce the need for women to go to work, by paying them to stay home and look after their children if there is no male breadwinner in the household. However, in 1967 Congress became alarmed at rising welfare rolls in the midst of a prosperous economy and enacted the Work Incentive Program (WIN) to provide training, job placement, and day care to help welfare recipients become self-supporting.[3]

At present, day care and early childhood programs are relatively small items in the federal budget. The Nixon administration's budget requests for fiscal 1973—the 12-month period beginning July 1, 1972—included about $1 billion for child care and related programs, about $100 million more than in fiscal 1973.[4] Most of the money is for day care of welfare children whose mothers work or receive job training and for the Head Start program, which provides pre-school education for children in poverty. These programs reach only a fraction of their potential participants.

If the federal government were to take on a major responsibility for day-care education and development, budgetary costs could mount rapidly. It was calculated in the Brookings study, for example, that operating a free public pre-school

---

[3] WIN and other programs funded under terms of Title 4A of the Social Security Act of 1967 required the government to pay 75 to 80 per cent of the child-care costs. The figure rises to 90 per cent on July 1, 1972. Title 4A expenditures amounted to $226 million in fiscal 1971 and served 570,000 children.

[4] The Senate Labor and Public Welfare Committee on May 16, 1972, approved a bill (S 3617) authorizing $2.95 billion in 1973-1975. See Congressional Quarterly *Weekly Report*, May 27, 1972, p. 1215.

program for all three- and four-year-olds at federal expense might cost about $5 billion a year—an estimate based on the assumption that three out of four eligible children would participate. Federal provision of free day care for children of low- and moderate-income families could easily cost $12 billion to $15 billion a year by 1977, the study added. That estimate assumes a 50 per cent participation by children under age 14 in families with incomes below the Labor Department's "lower living standard budget" ($7,214 for a family of four). It also assumes a cost of $2,000 per child through five years of age, and $700 a child for those six to 14 for care before and after school and during the summer.

Extent and Cost of Services Currently Available

A number of other estimates have been put forth for federal outlays required and per-child costs *(see p. 83)*. Calculations vary from $300 to $3,000 a year per child, a great gap explained partly by differences in the kinds of day care being considered. All three types of day care—custodial, developmental, and comprehensive—are offered by private and public, profit and non-profit organizations. In a survey conducted for the Office of Economic Opportunity (OEO) in 1970, the Westinghouse Learning Corp. counted 17,500 day-care centers that were licensed[5] and serving at least seven children. Half of them enrolled fewer than 30 children. About 60 per cent of the centers were proprietary,[6] run by individuals or companies for a profit. The rest were non-profit, operated by churches, community action agencies, charitable groups and the like, and in a few cases by public schools.

Westinghouse divided the programs into three categories, designated A, B and C, corresponding roughly to custodial, developmental and comprehensive *(see table, p. 73)*. Many of the category C centers were funded by Head Start and other federal programs.[7] In contrast, category A centers were mostly unsubsidized and offered much less costly service, primarily to lower middle-income families. The B centers served a

---

[5] Licensing is carried out by the states—by welfare departments in 36 states, health departments in five states, and another agency or combination of agencies in the remaining states. General requirements for licensing include the condition of the building, the amount of space available, staff-child ratios, health and safety regulations, and provision of adequate meals.

[6] Another study conducted for OEO found 90 per cent of all full-day centers operated in the United States to be privately operated for profit. See Irving Lazar and Mae E. Rosenberg, *Day Care: Resources for Decisions*, June 1971.

[7] Federal funds are available to state and local public agencies and to voluntary organizations that meet Federal Interagency Day Care Requirements. These standards relate to facilities, health and educational services, opportunities for parental involvement, staff qualifications and adult-child ratios.

slightly higher income group than the A centers but offered less costly services than C centers.

The National Council of Jewish Women evaluated the quality of care provided by the centers they studied, as follows:

	Non-profit	Proprietary
Good or superior	38%	15%
Fair	51	35
Poor	11	50

Half of the proprietary centers were rated poor and 35 per cent only fair. "In more than half the proprietary centers the size of classes exceeded accepted standards and the adult-child ratios were far too low," the council reported. "Salaries paid center directors and other professional staff were, on the whole, very much lower than those paid elementary school personnel.... The majority of staff were people with little or no training in early childhood education or development."

The most profit-oriented of the private day-care centers are the business chains and franchise operations. These centers, which charge from $20 to $50 a week per child, are geared to middle- and upper-income parents. "A dozen companies now operate over 100 day-care centers in 21 states; six of them alone say they will be caring for 50,000 children by the end of this year," Marion Meade wrote in the spring of 1971. "Suddenly millions of dollars have popped up in a crash attempt to cash in on a new industry. The new chain businesses and franchise operations have cute names (Mary Moppet, Kay's Kiddie Kollege, Les Petites Academies) and the brand new equipment invariably impresses nervous parents. But—can they successfully dish up kids the way they serve hamburger and fried chicken?"[8]

Less profit-minded are the companies and labor unions that have established day-care centers for the children of their women workers. The largest of the corporations operating these centers are affiliates of the American Telephone & Telegraph Co. AT&T, like a number of other companies, hopes that such services will reduce employee turnover and result in happier and more productive workers. The company pays half of the $30 weekly cost for each child. Charges for other business-sponsored centers are often based on ability to pay and range up to $25 a week. Fees for union-sponsored centers, like those of the Amalgamated Clothing Workers of America, come out of union dues.

---

[8] Marion Meade, "The Politics of Day Care," *Commonweal*, April 16, 1971, p. 134.

OPERATION OF DAY-CARE CENTERS

	A (Custodial)	B (Developmental)	C (Comprehensive)
Proprietary	79%	68%	17%
Community-action agencies	0	2	46
Churches	12	25	8
Other	9	5	29

SOURCE: Westinghouse Learning Corp. and Westat Research Inc., *Day Care Survey—1970: Summary Report and Basic Analysis* (prepared for the Office of Economic Opportunity)

In a message to Congress on Feb. 19, 1969, less than a month after he took office, President Nixon said "So crucial is the matter of early growth that we must make a national commitment to providing all American children an opportunity for healthful and stimulating development during the first five years of life." The administration and Congress have disagreed, however, over the form and size of the commitment. The administration continued to fund the Head Start program but moved it from OEO, the anti-poverty agency set up by the Johnson administration, to the newly created Office of Child Development in HEW. The major administration emphasis has been on day care as part of welfare reform.

Nixon's proposals for welfare reform were embodied in a Family Assistance Plan he outlined in a nationally televised address on Aug. 8, 1969. As stated, unemployed welfare recipients would be required to accept training or employment, or lose a portion of the benefits they would receive under other provisions of the plan. A major feature was the provision of day care for the children of welfare mothers who seek work or training. "The day care I propose is more than custodial," the President said in his message. "This administration is committed to a new emphasis on child development in the first five years of life. The day care that would be part of this plan would be of a quality that will help in the development of the child and provide for its health and safety, and would break the poverty cycle for this new generation."

Passage and Veto of Mondale Plan for Full Care

The administration proposals, as written into a bill titled Social Security Amendments of 1971 (HR 1), called for first-year spending of $750 million for day-care services and facilities, and an increase in income tax deductions to be claimed for child-care expenses paid by families earning less than

$12,000 a year. Congressional liberals, with the support of organized labor and many groups interested in child welfare, meanwhile pushed ahead with their own child-care plans, which they attached to the Economic Opportunity Amendments of 1971. The Senate version, sponsored by Sen. Walter F. Mondale (D Minn.), sought to provide comprehensive child development services for all children through age 14 —although priority would be given to children of families whose incomes fell below the Labor Department's definition of "minimum living standard" ($6,960 for a family of four). Sixty-five per cent of the spaces would be reserved for these children; the rest would be available to other children, whose fees would be determined by family income.

In an attempt to avoid a presidential veto, the House lowered the free-care cutoff point to $4,320, the eligibility line for a family of four to receive assistance under the proposed Family Assistance Plan. The lower figure was accepted on final congressional passage, but the measure was vetoed nevertheless. Nixon said in his veto message of Dec. 10, 1971, that the provisions were characterized by "fiscal irresponsibility, administrative unworkability and family-weakening implications." Among the presidential objections were these:

Workability. Allowing small communities to be prime sponsors would create administrative difficulties and relegate the states to an insignificant role.

Overlapping. Child care in some instances duplicated provisions of the Family Assistance Plan.

Tax deductions. Nixon pointed out that the Revenue Act of 1971 provided "a significant federal subsidy to day care...potentially benefiting 97 per cent of all families in the country." The act provided income-tax deductions up to $400 a month, beginning in 1972, for couples whose incomes did not exceed $18,000 a year. It also provided similar deductions for single parents or those treated as single for tax purposes.

Radical legislation. "I must share the view of those of its supporters who proclaim this to be the most radical piece of legislation to emerge from the 92nd Congress." Nixon further said it "would commit the vast moral authority of the national government to the side of communal approaches to child rearing against the family-centered approach."

There was also the question of expense. The original version of the Mondale bill proposed an expenditure of $2 billion the first year of operation, $4 billion the second year and $7 billion the third. Authorization for the second- and third-year amounts was dropped from the bill's final version. HR 1, in contrast, called for the allocation of $750 million in the first year.

A Senate attempt to override the veto fell seven votes short of the required two-thirds majority. Sens. Mondale and Gaylord Nelson (D Wis.), attempting to meet some of the President's objections, offered a revised bill which won the approval of the Senate Labor and Public Welfare Committee on May 3, 1972. Fee schedules remained similar to those in the vetoed bill but only $1.2 billion was requested for the first year of operation and full-day services would be restricted to children whose parents were already working and to handicapped children.

"If another bill passes Congress this year, President Nixon is sure to veto it again, and conservatives have the votes to sustain that veto," William V. Shannon of *The New York Times* editorial board wrote on April 30, 1972. "Over the long term, however, a bill bearing some resemblance to Mondale's is likely, sooner or later, to become law. The political arithmetic of the growing number of working mothers guarantees that."[9]

Sporadic Growth of Day-Care Services

THE FIRST AMERICAN day nursery for children of poor working mothers, the New York Nursery and Children's Hospital, began operations in 1854, admitting children from six weeks to six years of age. It was open from 6 a.m. to 7 p.m. to coincide with the mothers' working hours. The impetus behind the founding of this nursery and those which soon came to be established in other large cities was philanthropic. But as demand grew, especially among women widowed by the Civil War, a number of private individuals went into baby-sitting for profit. Beginning with Massachusetts in 1863, states set up boards of charity to inspect child-care facilities. In 1885, Pennsylvania became the first state to require licensing. Any person offering care to more than two children under the age of three had to obtain a license "from the mayor of the town or a justice of the peace or a magistrate of the locality."

By the end of the 19th century, the number of day-care centers—both proprietary and philanthropic—had grown substantially. Few of them offered more than custodial care, and child abuse and deprivation were far from uncommon. The

---

[9] "A Radical, Direct, Simple, Utopian Alternative to Day-Care Centers," *The New York Times Magazine*, April 30, 1972, p. 13.

National Federation of Day Nurseries was founded in 1898 to encourage the growth of day-care centers and to promote health and safety standards. Reports of continued mistreatment prompted the first White House Conference on the Care of Dependent Children, in 1909, to recommend that children be cared for in their own homes as far as possible, with charitable assistance limited to "reasonably efficient and deserving mothers who are without the support of a normal breadwinner." The White House Conference also urged the states to establish higher standards for the inspection and licensing of existing centers. The United States Children's Bureau took up this call after its establishment in 1912.

A great spurt in female employment during World War I greatly increased the need for day-care facilities, but no effective moves were made at that time to set up public nurseries. Their growth was held back by a prevailing view that group care was harmful to infants and small children. As late as 1930, according to a report made to that year's White House Conference on the Care of Dependent Children, there were only about 800 day-care establishments in the country, most of them in big cities or near industrial plants where large numbers of women were employed. Most mothers obliged to work preferred to hire other women to look after their children rather than to place them in a facility set up solely for child care. On the other hand, the day nursery was regarded as a better alternative than an institution that took permanent custody of the children, and for many working mothers the choice was one or the other.

Child-Study Centers and WPA Pre-School Projects

During the 1920s, when the effort to establish group-care facilities for children of working mothers was marking time, a movement to set up nursery schools with child-study centers for youngsters aged three to five became popular. The demand for nursery schools was stimulated by research in child development and by popularization of the research findings. Some of the earliest "laboratory" schools were established on college campuses before 1920. These included the Iowa Child Welfare Research Station at the University of Iowa and similar centers at Yale, Columbia and the University of Minnesota.

The two movements differed in key respects. The day-care center was regarded as a kind of necessary evil; its clientele were the unfortunates of society, and its primary purpose was to keep children clean, fed and safe. The nursery school, on the other hand, was looked upon as a positive boon to children, supplementing rather than substituting for the mother's care. Its clientele were from the middle and upper classes—families that could afford the relatively high cost of a facility that offered learning experiences beneficial to the child's mental and social development.

The day-care and nursery-school movements came together to some degree during the Depression Thirties when the Works Progress Administration (WPA) established facilities for the children of needy parents. Although the chief objective was to provide jobs for unemployed teachers and other adults, the WPA nurseries were also planned to help mothers who needed to work; the schools tried to give children of the poor some of the advantages of pre-school education that were available to the middle and upper classes in private nursery schools. Many of these WPA projects were operated under the direction of the public schools.

By 1936 the federal government was spending $6 million a year for day-care programs which, at their peak, enrolled 75,000 children in 1,900 centers.[10] When the WPA went out of existence in 1942, there were 39,000 children in 944 centers. Local authorities or groups of parents kept the centers going in some communities after federal aid was cut off, but their efforts were for the most part unsuccessful. The co-operative nursery school movement then gathered momentum, but it, like the pre-Depression child-study nurseries, was not oriented to the needs of children whose mothers were obliged to work.

Centers for Workers' Children in World War II

Soon after Pearl Harbor, it became apparent that child-care services would be urgently needed because of the influx of women into the wartime labor market. The Community Facilities (or Lanham) Act of 1941 was used as a vehicle for the allocation of federal funds directly to local communities to build and operate day-care centers for the children of war workers. The program reached its peak in July 1944 when 3,102 day-care centers were serving 130,000 children; these centers included full-day nurseries for pre-school children and after-school facilities for older children. When federal financial suport was withdrawn in March 1945, there were more than 2,000 of these nurseries enrolling about 70,000 pre-schoolers. During the entire period, a total of $52 million in federal

---

[10] Other federal programs for day care were sponsored by the Farm Security Administration, which maintained centers for the children of migrant farm workers. The 1937 Federal Housing Act provided loans for construction of community day-care facilities.

funds was allotted to projects in virtually every state; the federal funds were supplemented by $26 million in local contributions.

After federal money was cut off, only four states—California, Massachusetts, New York and Washington—made state funds available to keep day-care centers open. California's Children's Centers, operated by school districts and paid for by the state and parents' fees, were by far the most successful. A number of communities tried to operate programs without state or federal aid, but most of their efforts failed. In a number of cases, the centers remained open for a time, but the quality and scope of services declined.[11]

During the war, a few private concerns set up day-care centers for the children of their female employees. The most notable of these company-operated efforts were two centers in Portland, Ore., run by the Kaiser shipbuilding concern. Built in 1943 for children as young as 18 months, each center was open 24 hours a day and cared for about 375 children. The staff included 100 trained teachers, 10 nurses and several nutritionists. Parents paid $5 a week for one child and $3.75 for each additional child. The Kaiser centers operated for 20 months, served a total of 38,111 children and are generally credited with providing quality developmental care for their charges.

Popularity of Head Start; Questioning of Benefits

The 1962 amendments to the public welfare provisions of the Social Security Act made the first specific authorization of federal aid for child-care centers after World War II. The amount authorized—$5 million for fiscal 1963 and up to $10 million in succeeding years—was considered no more than a "drop in the bucket." Still, the legislation marked a recognition by the federal government of a sociological fact of life—that women in large numbers had entered the labor force, that they were there to stay, that many of them had children, and that the children would suffer lasting damage if they received poor care or no care while their mothers worked.

President Johnson's anti-poverty program, particularly the 1964 Economic Opportunity Act, encouraged the establishment of day-care services for the poor.[12] Probably the most successful of all the anti-poverty legislation has been Project

---

[11] See "Child Day Care and Working Mothers," *E.R.R.*, 1965 Vol. II, pp. 490-491.
[12] The act also provided funds for day care through the Concentrated Employment Program, which authorized day-care funds in connection with manpower training programs and the Migrant Children's Program.

Head Start, a service which recalls the nursery school programs of WPA days. Head Start was launched in the summer of 1965 to assist pre-school children from deprived families. Parental involvement was strongly encouraged. The original Head Start summer program was so successful that President Johnson announced a substantial expansion in 1965, including the establishment of year-round centers.

Head Start's main objective is to overcome the educational, medical and social handicaps which hold back many poor children when they enter the public schools. According to the Office of Child Development, 274,000 children were enrolled in 1,147 full-year programs and 117,000 in 614 summer programs in fiscal 1971. The cost to the federal government was $360 million. The report of the National Council of Jewish Women on day-care facilities was enthusiastic about Head Start programs and strongly recommended that they be continued and expanded.

However, one major assumption underlying the Head Start program has been challenged in recent years. It is the belief that the children of the poor, many of them black, tend to fall behind in measurable intelligence because of an unstimulating environment in their formative years. Accumulating evidence seems to suggest that pre-school programs can raise scores on intelligence tests several points but that these gains tend to fade after the children enter regular school. "Compensatory education has been tried and it apparently has failed," Arthur R. Jensen, professor of educational psychology at the University of California at Berkeley, wrote in 1969. Those opening words of a scholarly paper[13] brought to a boil a simmering dispute in the academic community over the relative value of heredity and environment in childhood learning. The issue is still being debated.

Problems and Prospects for Child Care

IN RECENT YEARS, American child development experts have looked closely and often enviously at day-care programs of other countries. Dr. James Comer of the Yale University

---

[13] Arthur R. Jensen, "How Much Can We Boost I.Q. and Scholastic Achievement," *Harvard Educational Review*, winter 1969. For further discussion, see "Human Intelligence," *E.R.R.*, 1969 Vol. II, pp. 617-620, and Richard Herrnstein, "I.Q.," *Atlantic*, September 1969.

USERS OF DAY-CARE CENTERS

	Custodial	Developmental	Comprehensive
Families with income under $4,000	18%	16%	59%
Families with income of $4,000 to $8,000	54	39	24
Families with income over $8,000	28	45	17

SOURCE: Westinghouse Learning Corp. and Westat Research Inc., *Day Care Survey—1970: Summary Report and Basic Analysis* (prepared for the Office of Economic Opportunity)

Child Study Center in New Haven, testifying at Senate hearings in 1971, gave the following description of child care in Sweden:

> In Stockholm, there are supervised parks, so that when children come to play in the park, there are adults there to provide for the supervision they need. The day-care centers are available to a vast number of people. They feel they do not have enough, and yet what they have is far more than we provide for our children....[14]

In France, the first western nation to establish a free preschool system for the children of working mothers in 1887, every community with a population of more than 2,000 is required today to have an *école maternelle* for children up to age six. And most French cities also provide a *crèche* for infants as young as two months. Enrollment in the former had reached two million in 1971, up from 650,000 in 1955. "The prevailing French philosophy is that no mother—working or otherwise—is able to give her child sufficient intellectual stimulation, so teachers are trained not only in the basics of child care, but in psychomotor development, linguistics, music, bilingual experimentation and new math."[15]

Some American authorities have praised those aspects of day care in Communist countries that are not ideological. In Cuba, 50,000 children under age six are reported to be cared for in 450 centers. In contrast, New York City, with a population equal to Cuba's, has only 18,000 children enrolled in day care. According to two American observers, "Cuba spends a larger percentage of its Gross National Product on day care than almost any other country in the world... The centers operate

---

[14] Testimony at joint hearings conducted by the Subcommittee on Employment, Manpower and Poverty, and the Subcommittee on Children and Youth, units of the Senate Labor and Public Welfare Committee, May 26, 1971.

[15] "Day Care? In France It's a Science," *The New York Times,* Dec. 20, 1970.

year-round and provide free care, including clothing and all meals during school hours."[16]

In the Soviet Union, roughly one-third of the 30 million preschool children are enrolled either in nurseries for children from two months to three years or in kindergartens for youngsters aged 3-7. There is some indication that while most Russian mothers are satisfied with the kindergarten services, many are less than happy about placing very young children in Soviet nurseries. The number of children under three in Moscow nurseries has fallen off in recent years.[17]

Israel offers the most novel and publicized child-care services of any nation, East or West. These services are of two basic types: (1) day-care centers for the children of working mothers, similar to but more numerous and extensively used than those in the United States, and (2) communal childrearing settlements in the kibbutz. From birth, kibbutz children live in separate houses with their own age group. A specially trained caretaker and her assistant are usually in charge of six to eight youngsters. However, mothers spend a substantial amount of time with their children, especially during the first two years of life. "The collective rearing of children actually frees the kibbutz mother to devote her time more exclusively with her own child. It would be difficult to imagine a city mother, employed or not, who could spend an unhampered play period with her child as a matter of daily routine."[18]

Demands of Women for More and Better Services

The Westinghouse survey found that more than 350,000 working mothers in families with incomes under $8,000 were very dissatisfied with their child-care arrangements. Some 750,-000 others at this income level said lack of day-care service was an obstacle to employment.[19] Many of these women had family incomes above the level which would allow them to qualify for federally subsidized programs but below that needed to afford comprehensive private services. These mothers of the poor and "near poor" who work or want to work because of economic necessity have been joined in their demands for child-care services by their middle-income sisters. At the White

[16] Marvin Leiner and Robert Ubell, "Children are the Revolution," *Saturday Review*, April 1, 1972, pp. 54-58.

[17] "Moscow Is Split on Nursery Issue," *The New York Times*, March 21, 1971.

[18] Hava Bonne Gerwitz, "Child Care Facilities and the 'Israeli Experience'," *Day Care: Resources for Decisions* (1971), pp. 44-46.

[19] Janice N. Hedges and Jeanne K. Barnett, "Working Women and the Division of Household Tasks," *Monthly Labor Review*, April 1972, p. 12.

PERCENTAGE OF AMERICAN MOTHERS WHO HOLD JOBS

Year	All mothers	With children under age 6	With children 6-17 years old
1950	22	14	33
1960	30	20	43
1970	42	32	52

SOURCE: Labor Department

House Conference on Children, held in December 1970, women denounced government policies that limited day care to welfare recipients. Women's liberationists insisted that child care be divorced from public assistance and made available to any mother who wants it.

In a statement issued May 18, 1971, the National Organization for Women (Now) argued that "widespread availability of child-care facilities is essential if women are to have a true choice of life styles..."

> Women will never have full opportunity to participate in America's economic, political, or cultural life [the statement continued] as long as they bear the sole responsibility for the care of children—entirely alone and isolated from the larger world...Child care benefits children and the family just as much as the woman. A child whose environment is limited to his or her own small family unit cannot thrive.

Demand for greatly expanded or universal day care is by no means limited to committed or radical feminists. Women in the Ripon Society, a liberal Republican research and policy group, threatened to set up a separate caucus when the organization supported President Nixon's child-care veto. George F. Gelder, editor of the society's *Ripon Forum,* responded:

> Why is comprehensive day care so urgently demanded by the woman's movement? The answer, I venture, lies in the ambivalence of many upper-income women toward the options of liberation... These women's guilts and anxieties are akin to those felt by many wealthy people about all their advantages... A 'meaningful' and uninterrupted career is generally the privilege of mothers with money and education....If day care is universal, they can imagine that their liberation is not a perquisite of affluence but a democratic 'human right'....

"These upper-class women perfer not to acknowledge that their less fortunate sisters would be manumitted to mops and switchboards; that day care would be used by the government in part to facilitate compulsory labor; that for most women caring for one's own child is more 'meaningful' than attending to an assembly line...."[20]

Probably the most controversial issue in the debate on child care is its effect on very young children. Vast numbers of studies have shown that the years from birth to about age three are crucial in the intellectual, physical and psychological development of children. Earlier research stressed what appeared to be the bad effects on an infant or young child of separation from the mother. More recent studies indicate the deleterious effects observed resulted from the kind of impersonal care given in institutions rather than from any inherent fault in group care. The newer studies made a distribution between mother-deprivation and mother-separation: A child deprived of normal maternal affection suffers ill effects, but separation from a normally loving mother for part of the day does not denote maternal deprivation and can actually be beneficial to both the young child and its mother.

Financial Barriers to Expansion of Child Care

The greatest immediate impediment to quality day care is not so much the sociological or psychological fears that it may endanger the family structure or damage young children but the fact that it is expensive. A study made by Jule Sugarman and Lawrence Feldman in 1968 for HEW gave the following estimates of the costs of day care per child per year:

	Minimum	Acceptable	Desirable
Day-care center (pre-schooler)	$1,245	$1,862	$2,320
Family day care (to age six)	1,423	2,032	2,372
Before and after school	310	653	653

The "minimum" standard was defined as care sufficient to maintain the health and safety of the child, with little attention to his development. "Acceptable" quality included a "basic program of developmental activities" in addition to custodial care, while "desirable" included a broader range of services, including health care and parent education.

In contrast to the foregoing costs, one researcher has concluded on the basis of survey evidence: "It can be expected that fewer than 5 per cent of all families...will pay over $20 per week per child and fewer than 1 per cent...would pay $40 a week....Families ordinarily will not pay more than 20-30 per cent of family incomes for child care for all children."[21] Clearly,

---

[20] "The Case Against Universal Day Care," *New Leader,* April 3, 1972, p. 13.

[21] Mary P. Rowe, "The Economics of Child Care," in *Child Care* (hearings before the Senate Finance Committee, 1971), p. 270.

the bulk of financial assistance for future day-care services must come from public sources, principally the federal government.

In the absence of any large-scale federal spending for child care, several proposals have been put forth to meet the costs. Ina G. Berman, a consultant to the Community Coordinated Child Care program in Boston, has suggested that the taxpayer finance day-care centers in the same way he finances the public schools.[22] At present school financing is borne largely by local property taxation. Patricia G. Bourne, writing in *The New Republic,* Feb. 12, 1972, proposed linking wage stability with free day care. "When the Scandinavians were faced with the problem of limiting wages in order to maintain a competitive position in the world economy, they substituted social benefits, which generate activity in the economy without inflationary stress, for wage increases. Free or subsidized child-care services seen as substitutes for wage increases might be politically acceptable."

One of the simplest solutions was proposed by Dr. Benjamin Spock in his best-selling book, *Baby and Child Care.* The controversial pediatrician wrote: "It would save money in the end if the government paid a comfortable allowance to all mothers of young children who would otherwise be compelled to work." William V. Shannon agrees with Spock's conclusion. "A comparison of costs suggests that the federal government, if it chooses to do so, can as easily pay a mother to take care of her own children as to finance them in a day-care facility."[23]

Shannon calls this a "radical, direct, simple, utopian alternative to day care centers." Women's liberationists, mothers who would rather work outside the home, federal budgetmakers, and a number of educators and child psychologists would doubtless disagree. Arguments about the value or danger of group care for children, about the best type of service and about whether the government should encourage or provide child care for all or only for the poor can be expected to continue in the years to come. And while the debate goes on, the number of working mothers and the number of children needing care will be growing.

---

[22] Reported by Susan Hunsinger in the *Christian Science Monitor*, Dec. 29, 1969.

[23] The Brookings authors wrote: "A state that pays a welfare mother with three children $60 a week is, in effect, purchasing day care for $20 a week, which is less than it would cost to take care of the child in a good non-profit day-care center. If such a mother participated in a training program and found a job that paid $90 a week, she might be able to support herself without welfare assistance, but she would not be able to contribute much to the costs of child care."

CRIME OF RAPE

by

Helen B. Shaffer

RISING AWARENESS OF RAPE IN AMERICA
Big Statistical Increase During the Past Decade
'Women's Lib' Criticism of Handling Complaints
Physical and Psychological Damage to the Victim

SEXUAL AGGRESSION AND AGGRESSORS
Patterns of Prevalence by Area, Age and Race
Modern Conditions That Encourage Sex Attacks
Ghetto Violence and Question About Pornography
Jekyll-Hyde Personality of the Rapist-Murderer
Other Aggressors; Homosexual Assaults in Prison

LEGAL DEALINGS WITH SEXUAL OFFENSES
Police Investigations: Sympathy and Skepticism
Pivotal Question of Woman's Sexual 'Innocence'
Death, Imprisonment and Treatment for Rapists
Varied Advice to Women for Their Self-Defense

1 9 7 2
Jan. 19

CRIME OF RAPE

RAPE, THE CRIME most feared by women, appears to be on the increase and no one is quite sure what to do about it. Apprehending the rapist is difficult, and convicting him even more difficult. The rapist apparently comes in many guises: he may be a deranged sadist, an alienated youth who casually assaults a woman as an adjunct to petty theft, a mild-mannered family man driven periodically to rape and kill, or just an ardent fellow who mistook his petting partner's "no" for "yes."

Women's liberationists complain that the police do not take rape charges as seriously as they should unless the woman can show bruises, cuts or other unmistakable evidence of physical abuse. The police, on the other hand, are in a dilemma as they try to separate valid complaints from the false. For if rape is the hardest crime to prove, it is also the easiest to fake.

Rape is unique among the crimes of violence. It is the only one in which the criminal factor is not the act itself—but whether the victim was forced to participate. If the act is performed without her consent, it is rape; if it is with her consent—and she is an adult—there is no offense.[1] A man may be the innocent victim of a false rape charge, just as a woman may be the innocent victim of a rapist who claims she was a willing participant in the sexual act. Since witnesses are rarely present, the case becomes a matter of balancing the credibility of the complainant with the credibility of the alleged attacker.

The only statistical count of the number of forcible rapes[2] in the United States is derived from reports of police departments to the Federal Bureau of Investigation, which collates the information and includes the results in its annual publica-

---

[1] Except in rare cases the charge of fornication may be filed in jurisdictions where there are still laws forbidding sexual intercourse outside of wedlock. Legally, a wife cannot be raped by her husband.

[2] The term used by the FBI in its crime reports to categorize an attack on a woman to force coitus on her against her will. It excludes statutory rape—sexual intercourse with a willing under-age girl. Seven out of 10 forcible rape reports in 1970 were of a completed rape; the others were "attempts or assaults to commit forcible rape."

tion titled *Uniform Crime Reports.* These summaries showed a 121 per cent increase in the number of forcible rapes that occurred from 1960 through 1970. An interim report issued on Sept. 29, 1971, showed a further increase in the first six months of 1971. The 37,270 cases reported in 1970 meant that forcible rape occurred in the United States on the average of every 14 minutes. Thirty-six of every 100,000 females in the nation, according to these statistics, were victims during the year of rape or assaults to commit rape. The "risk rate" for women increased 95 per cent over the 1960-70 decade. Except for a few years after the end of World War II, the rape rate has risen steadily since the early 1930s.

While the annual police reports are useful, it is generally understood that they do not begin to measure the actual prevalence of this crime in the nation. "Law enforcement administrators recognize," the FBI said, "that this offense is probably one of the most under-reported crimes."[3] The agency attributed the under-reporting "primarily to fear and/or embarrassment on the part of the victims." Fear and embarrassment, however, may not tell the whole story of the reluctance of women to report the crime. Interrogation by police, medical examination often by a doctor unknown to them for the purpose of obtaining evidence, confrontation with the rapist or other suspects, cross-examination by defense counsel —all of these may add up to an experience almost as traumatic as the ordeal of rape itself.

The degree of under-reporting was indicated in a survey conducted by the National Opinion Research Center, University of Chicago, at the request of the National Commission on the Causes and Prevention of Violence.[4] The center inquired of 10,000 households across the nation whether any member had been a victim of violent crime in 1965 and whether the crime had been reported. This survey, and others, suggested that the true rate may be three to four times higher than police figures show.

A staff report prepared for the commission emphasized, however, that there had been no validation of the claims of rape turned up during the survey. The staff was also uncertain whether there had been a genuine upswing in the incidence or merely more reporting of the crime. The commission's

---

[3] U.S. Department of Justice, Federal Bureau of Investigation, *Uniform Crime Reports—1970*, p. 14.

[4] The commission, which was headed by Dr. Milton S. Eisenhower, chairman, was created by President Johnson in June 1968 shortly after the murder of Sen. Robert F. Kennedy. It issued its final report in December 1969.

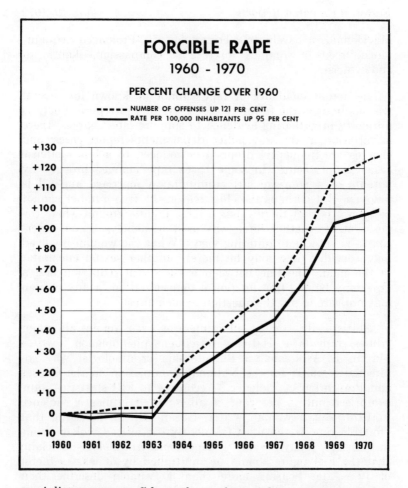

FORCIBLE RAPE
1960 - 1970

PER CENT CHANGE OVER 1960

- - - - - NUMBER OF OFFENSES UP 121 PER CENT
————— RATE PER 100,000 INHABITANTS UP 95 PER CENT

specialists were confident that other violent crimes had increased, but they said "conclusions on rape are difficult to make."[5]

'Women's Lib' Criticism of Handling Complaints

This attitude of skepticism on the credibility of women who claim they were raped runs generally through most of the accounts, professional or otherwise, dealing with this crime. The skepticism exasperates women's liberation leaders—and rape victims—who think it reflects a pervasive masculine attitude of suspicion toward women as well as tolerance of a certain degree of male sexual aggression, perhaps more than is acceptable to many women. "A dispassionate approach to the problem of rape is not easily obtained," writes John M.

---

[5] *Crimes of Violence*, Vol. 11 (a staff report submitted to the National Commission on the Causes and Prevention of Violence, December 1969), pp. 19-20, 59.

MacDonald, a psychiatrist-criminologist. "Prolonged acquaintance breeds a complex mixture of compassion, skepticism and cynicism."[6]

The actual incidence of rape cannot be known for several reasons besides the failure of some victims to report. There is difficulty in gathering evidence to support rape charges; there is variation in the way police departments report cases; and charges are frequently dropped or reduced to a lesser offense easier to prosecute. In some cases rape charges brought by parents of a teen-age girl culminate in marriage and all is forgiven. But perhaps the chief reason the true number cannot be known is that there exists a large middle ground where the question of whether force was used to achieve sexual intercourse is subject to differing views. What the woman involved may consider rape may be merely another sexual encounter to the man. The line between a successful seduction and a rape may be too fine for police determination. Many women may not care to put the question to such a test.

"Statistically, among all crimes, or even among all major crimes, rape is a relatively infrequent phenomenon," writes Marvin E. Wolfgang, a Philadelphia criminologist who co-directed research for the National Commission on the Causes and Prevention of Violence.[7] According to FBI statistics, rape comprised only 5 per cent of all reported crimes of violence in 1970. But a woman writer, Susan Griffin, asserting that "forcible rape is the most frequently committed violent crime in America today," said "independent criminologists" claim that the FBI figure should be multiplied by at least a factor of 10.[8] After hearing more than 30 women describe their ordeal during a "Speak-Out on Rape," organized by the Radical Feminists in New York in January 1971, another woman writer said that the true extent of the occurrence of rape is not realized because "women who are threatened with rape usually succumb, seldom scream, rarely report it and almost never see their assailants convicted."[9]

Physical and Psychological Damage to Victim

Regardless of its actual incidence, rape will always command special attention. It takes the report of only a very few rapes in a particular area to set off waves of tension and fear, causing women to restrict their normal activities and creating

---

[6] John M. MacDonald, *Rape: Offenders and Their Victims* (1971), p. 3.
[7] Foreword to *Patterns in Forcible Rape* (1971), by Menachem Amir.
[8] Susan Griffin: "Rape: The All-American Crime," *Ramparts*, September 1971, p. 27.
[9] Gail Sheehy, "Nice Girls Don't Get Into Trouble," *New York*, Feb. 15, 1971, p. 26.

an atmosphere of suspicion and even hysteria. The nature of the crime itself is peculiarly offensive to civilized people. "What is viewed as important by a society is not judged only by frequency of occurrence," Wolfgang wrote. "A sexual assault on a victim who gives no consent...is perceived as an impediment to personal choice."

The hurt inflicted is deep. Rape not only inflicts pain, terror and humiliation for the duration of the attack, but often causes lasting physical and psychological damage to the victim. Venereal disease, pregnancy, and emotional maladjustment may follow. Of 1,487 women raped in Washington, D.C., at least 63 became infected with venereal disease and nine became pregnant; a study in Denver showed that pregnancy followed for six out of 200 victims.[10] The psychic damage is more subtle and may not manifest itself for some time after the assault. Psychiatrists have observed that often sexual assaults are revealed in the case histories of seriously disturbed patients. The state of mind subsequent to rape is described by Dr. Seymour Halleck, chief psychiatrist of the Wisconsin Division of Corrections and member of the University of Wisconsin faculty:

> She is uncertain as to her role as a woman and such a role does appear to her at that moment as a degraded and helpless one. She wonders if she will again be attracted to men, or interested in normal sexual relations.
>
> A wide variety of pathological reactions may result following sexual assault. Women with previously vulnerable personalities are likely to develop neurotic symptoms, including anxiety attacks, phobias, hypochondrias, or depression.[11]

Even a previously well-adjusted woman can become disturbed as a result of rape. "It is indeed difficult to conceive of any woman going through this experience without developing some symptoms," Dr. Halleck said. Even if she escapes the rapist "the imminence of harm perceived by a woman on whom forcible rape is attempted can have deep psychological impact."

In a strange twist of the human psyche, many women suffer guilt feelings after being raped. "[The victim] may be tortured with self-accusation.... Often she blames herself for having neglected a minor defensive effort," Dr. Halleck wrote. Every one of the women who testified at the Speak-Out on Rape "suffered from the private conclusion that in some way it must

---

[10] Cited by MacDonald, *op. cit.*, p. 92. More than a dozen states permit abortion if the woman can prove she was raped. See "Abortion Law Reform," *E.R.R.*, 1970 Vol. II, p. 547.

[11] Seymour Halleck, "Emotional Effects of Victimization," in *Sexual Behavior and the Law* (1965), Ralph Slovenko, ed., p. 673.

have been her fault," reported Susan Griffin, who attributed this to the way women are conditioned in society.

Most damaging and most outrageous in the public mind is the forcible rape of a child or an inexperienced adolescent. Not only is there more likelihood of physical damage in the genital area, but the psychological impact is profound and may prevent normal maturation. "The child is unequipped to understand the sexual experience," wrote Dr. Halleck, "and consequently is likely to view it in a distorted way.... [She] is not yet ready to integrate sexual impulses with mature modes of interpersonal relationships and may develop distorted emotional responses." This can produce serious problems in later life, "ranging from frigidity with fear of intercourse to a type of aimless promiscuity...[without] sexual gratification."

Most sexual offenses against children fortunately do not go beyond fondling, and in most cases the child's compliance is won without resort to force. Out of roughly 18,000 interviews conducted by the Institute for Sex Research, no man or woman reported having been victimized as a child by a sadist. "Child murders in connection with sexual activity receive great publicity, which gives the impression that they are not infrequent; actually they are extremely rare." The murder may be an unintentional consequence of force used to subdue a resisting victim or it may follow "from a combination of guilt and panic" after the rape and as an effort to prevent detection. "By and large, the picture of the aggressor against children is one of alcoholism or heavy sporadic drinking, mental pathology or defect, and very low socioeconomic status."[12]

Sexual Aggression and Aggressors

ANY FEMALE may be a victim of rape. Lack of sexual attractiveness is no protection. Children barely out of infancy, women in advanced pregnancy and female octogenarians have been victims of sexual attack. Rapists often climb in bedroom windows or lie in wait for a chance victim in an apartment-house laundry room. But rape may occur anywhere, often in unexpected places. One offender scaled a convent wall in Brooklyn and attacked a nun. Another carried a hospital patient from her bed. "Rape of patients by hospital staff

---

[12] Paul Gebhard et al., *Sex Offenders* (1965), p. 151.

or by other patients occurs with more frequency than is generally recognized," John M. MacDonald wrote. Some rapists develop a smooth technique for getting women to admit them into their homes. Others cruise around looking for female hitch-hikers.

College dormitories and public schools may provide rapists with opportunities for assault. Protection against rape is by no means an unfamiliar subject at inner-city parent-teacher meetings. After several teachers in New York were raped in 1971, the city promised to add guards to the existing patrol force in high-risk schools. A Bronx teacher who had been raped initiated legal proceedings against the city, demanding $2 million in damages.

No area of the country is free of rape but the hazard is greatest in urban centers. Cities of 250,000 population or more account for 45 per cent of the forcible rapes reported to the FBI. The risk rate in big cities in 1970 was 77 per 100,000 females, compared with 25 in the suburbs and 19 in rural areas. However the rural rate has been climbing too; the FBI found a 5 per cent rise over the past decade. Though the South has more reported rapes than other major regions, the rape rate was highest in the West—56 per 100,000 women compared with 35 in the southern, 33 in the north central, and 25 in the northeastern states.

Rape may take place at any time of day or any day of the week. Nights and weekends, however, are the times of highest incidence. The Denver study of 200 rape cases indicated that from 10 p.m. to 4 a.m. on Saturday and Sunday was the most likely time for rape to occur; more than one-half of the 200 cases occurred in that time period. Similar findings were obtained from studies made in Philadelphia and in Denmark. Although most rapes take place indoors, the street is likely to be the place of first meeting between offender and victim. Of 143 women in the Denver study who were raped by men unknown to them, 70 were seized or enticed on the street and taken elsewhere to be raped. Twenty-three were attacked while getting in or out of their cars or while stopped for a traffic light or car trouble. One woman was raped by a "good Samaritan" who helped her fix a stalled car.

Most rapists are young. Of 445 cases of forcible rape cited in a national sampling of police cases, 93 (21 per cent) were age 17 or younger and only 138 (31 per cent) were 26 or older.[13]

---

[13] *Crimes of Violence*, p. 212.

The greatest concentration of arrests for rape in 1970 was among 17-20 year olds, the FBI reported; 64 per cent were under 25. Teen-agers account for much of the rate increase. While all rape arrests increased 55 per cent between 1960 and 1970, arrests of males under 18 increased 85 per cent. Arrest records also show a predominance of rapists among those in the lower ranks of society. The national sampling showed 27 per cent of the rapists were laborers and 8 per cent were unemployed.

Forty per cent of those arrested for forcible rape in 1970 were Negro, the FBI reported. Most studies of police records show that both the offender and victim are likely to be of the same race. Studies made for the National Commission on the Causes and Prevention of Violence indicated that 90 per cent of the rape cases were intraracial; in 60 per cent both offender and victim were black. In a vast majority of the inter-racial rape cases, the assailant was black and the victim white.

Modern Conditions That Encourage Sex Attacks

There are no historical studies of rape. But that rape has an ancient history is obvious from the frequency of the theme in myth, literature and art. Women have traditionally been considered legitimate booty for the victorious warrior and rape is still not uncommon under wartime conditions. One of the atrocity stories of the Viet Nam War dealt with rape-murder.[14] Whether rape occurs more or less frequently today than in previous periods of history cannot be determined.

The girl hitch-hiker, the woman driving her car, the secretary or widow living alone in an apartment, the teen-age baby-sitter alone in a house except for sleeping children—all these conditions present opportunities for rape that would not have been available in the past. On the other hand, girls today are less likely to be victimized by their employers in the way housemaids and shop girls were in the Victorian era. And there is no knowing how many rapes took place on the lawless frontier in a still-earlier period. If historians are correct in saying that violence was endemic to America's beginnings, it is unlikely that rape would not be among the forms that violence took.[15]

A loosening of sex morals might be thought to provide voluntary substitutes for forced partners in sex, but actually it may encourage some men to commit rape. A sociologist has suggested that the high rate of forcible rape in Los Angeles—

---

[14] Daniel Lang. *Incident on Hill 192* (1970), an account of the capture of a Viet Nam girl to serve the sexual needs of four American soldiers during patrol duty and of her subsequent murder to prevent discovery.

[15] See "Violence in American Life," *E.R.R.*, 1968 Vol. I, pp. 405-424.

RAPE RATES IN SELECTED
METROPOLITAN AREAS, 1970

(national average 18.3)

Metropolitan area	Number of rapes per 100,000 pop.	Metropolitan area	Number of rapes per 100,000 pop.
Akron	25.3	Louisville	21.1
Albuquerque	39.3	Memphis	27.9
Atlanta	21.7	Miami	17.0
Baltimore	34.9	Milwaukee	8.3
Baton Rouge	36.1	Minneapolis-St. Paul	16.8
Birmingham	21.4	Nashville	21.6
Boston-Lowell-Lawrence	14.8	Newark	20.5
Buffalo	13.7	New Orleans	41.7
Charleston, S.C.	35.2	New York	19.9
Charlotte	23.0	Oklahoma City	21.8
Chicago	25.4	Omaha	16.8
Cleveland	18.7	Philadelphia	15.2
Columbus	34.7	Phoenix	31.1
Dallas	41.0	Pittsburgh	14.0
Denver	49.7	Portland, Ore.	22.6
Detroit	31.1	Richmond	24.9
Hartford-New Britain-Bristol	10.9	St. Louis	34.4
Honolulu	13.5	Salt Lake City	14.3
Houston	27.1	San Antonio	28.1
Indianapolis	33.5	San Diego	19.4
Jersey City	9.8	San Francisco-Oakland	42.9
Kansas City	46.5	Seattle-Everett	23.8
Las Vegas	23.8	Syracuse	10.1
Little Rock-North Little Rock	48.9	Tampa-St. Petersburg	20.2
Los Angeles-Long Beach	50.0	Washington, D.C.	23.0

SOURCE: Federal Bureau of Investigation.

---

roughly one rape for every 100 women in 1970—might be due in part to the city's reputation as a place of considerable sexual freedom. Gilbert Geis of the University of California at Irvine, who has made a study of comparative rape rates, writes: "It is likely that a city which holds out to males the prospect for relatively free access to females probably induces more frustration as a consequence of denied expectation and ultimately has higher rape rates than a city in which there is lesser expectation of sexual success."[16] Many commentators on this problem point out that males often assume that if a

[16] "More Rape in Los Angeles Than Boston," *Sexual Behavior*, November 1971, p. 35. See also "Sexual Revolution: Myth or Reality," *E.R.R.*, 1970 Vol. I, pp. 241-258.

woman acts in a seductive way or indicates by speech or manner that she is a "free woman" she becomes fair game, even if she balks at intercourse with someone not of her own choice.

Ghetto Violence and Question About Pornography

Some rapes are a manifestation of the social disorganization and epidemic violence of city slums. "The urban ghetto produces a subculture...in which violence is accepted as normative and natural in everyday life, not necessarily illicit," according to the Violence Commission's staff study. A criminolgist's description of a new type of criminal behavior—crime "for sport," marked by indifference to the moral judgments of society—may have relevance to rape as it occurs today.[17]

Experts disagree on whether pornography, especially when it combines sex and violence, encourages rape. Two presidential commissions seemed to take different stands on this question. The Violence Commission said in 1969 that violence portrayed by the media can induce aggression, while the Commission on Obscenity and Pornography said a year later that studies provided "no evidence that exposure to or use of explicit sexual materials play a significant role in the causation of...crime, delinquency, sexual or non-sexual deviancy or severe emotional disturbances." Commenting on the two commission reports, a University of Wisconsin psychologist said: "What bothers me is the possibility, admittedly very slight but still not zero, that a small number of persons might be instigated to obtain their sexual pleasures through unwilling victims."[18] Susan Griffin has complained that the culture encourages rape because it conditions the man to be aggressive and the woman passive.

What motivates the rapist? To answer that he rapes to satisfy his sexual urge is not enough. Many rapists are married[19] or are men with no particular problem finding sexual partners. Rapists have been known to turn down an offer from a willing woman, preferring to seek an unwilling one. A black rapist may seek a white woman to vent his rage against white oppression, justifying the act as vengeance for black women raped by white men in the days of slavery. Eldridge Cleaver, the black militant leader, thus explained his past as a rapist:

[17] See George W. Crockett Jr., "New Crimes for Old," *American Scholar*, Autumn 1971, p. 584.

[18] Leonard Berkowitz, "Sex and Violence: We Can't Have It Both Ways," *Psychology Today*, December 1971, pp. 14.

[19] Three out of five rapists interviewed by researchers of the (Kinsey) Institute for Sex Research at Indiana University were married. Other studies show 40-43 per cent married. See Paul Gebhard et. al., *Sexual Offenders* (1965), and John M. MacDonald, *op. cit.*, p. 55.

INCIDENCE OF RAPE IN AMERICA

Year	Number of rapes per 100,000 pop.	Year	Number of rapes per 100,000 pop.
1935	4.4	1955	8.0
1940	5.3	1960	9.4
1945	8.9	1965	11.9
1950	7.3	1970	18.3

SOURCE: Federal Bureau of Investigation.

"Somehow I arrived at the conclusion that, as a matter of principle, it was of paramount importance for me to have an antagonistic, ruthless attitude toward white women.... Rape was an insurrectionary act. It delighted me that I was defying ...the white man's law...and..defiling his women.... I felt I was getting revenge." Later he "took a long look" at himself and admitted he was wrong. "I could not approve the act of rape.... I lost my self-respect."[20]

Jekyll-Hyde Personality of the Rapist-Murderer

The most dangerous kind of rapist—the potential killer— is the sadist who seeks sexual satisfaction by inflicting cruelty. The fear and powerlessness of his victim are necessary to his sexual pleasure or even his capability for coitus. Some sadists are unable to complete the act and inflict various forms of painful sexual abuse on the woman. One-fourth of the convicted "heterosexual aggressors against adults" interviewed by Kinsey researchers[21] were of this type.

Psychiatrists attribute the behavior of such men to a deep-seated hostility to women, rooted in a faulty childhood relationship with their mothers. These men are usually loners who make little or no effort to win a woman's compliance, frequently use weapons to threaten or punish her, and select the victim without regard for her appearance. Moreover, the rape is often accompanied by some form of petty theft. They have a predilection for strangling their victims. Strangulation not only chokes off cries; it also gives the attacker a sense of power. "By increasing or decreasing pressure he can give or take away life," British psychiatrist Robert P. Brittain wrote.[22] Victims often show multiple stab wounds.

[20] Eldridge Cleaver, *Soul on Ice* (1968), pp. 13-15.

[21] Dr. Alfred C. Kinsey, with two colleagues, wrote the pioneer work, *Sexual Behavior in the Human Male* (1948). Kinsey died in 1956. His research into human sexual behavior is being carried on by the Institute for Sex Research at Indiana University.

[22] Robert P. Brittain, "The Sadistic Murder," *Medicine, Science and the Law*, October 1970, p. 198.

Sadist-murderers may be difficult to identify. They "may appear to be much like other people," Brittain added. "No one should be ruled out as a suspect...even close relatives may have little idea of his abnormalities." The man identified as the "Boston Strangler" was a mild-mannered father of two who could not explain why he was driven to grab unsuspecting women from the rear, choke them, try to rape them, and then leave their bodies in grotesquely obscene positions.[23] The classic picture of brutality, neglect and distorted parent-child relations appeared in his case history.

Other Aggressors; Homosexual Assaults in Prison

In their study of sex offenders, Kinsey researchers categorized the following types of "sexual aggressors":

> *Amoral rapist.* Such men are not sadistic. "They simply want to have coitus and the females' wishes are of no particular consequence." While they are not hostile to women, they will use force, threat, or physical punishment if the woman tries to thwart them.

> *Drunken aggressor.* His aggression may range "from uncoordinated grapplings and pawings, which he construes as efforts at seduction, to hostile and truly vicious behavior released by intoxication."

> *Explosive type.* These are "men whose prior lives offer no surface indications of what is to come. Sometimes they are average, law-abiding citizens, sometimes...criminals, but their aggression appears suddenly, and, at the time, inexplicably." The stereotype of the explosive variety is "the mild straight-A high school student who suddenly rapes and kills."

> *Double-standard male.* He divides women into good and bad, treats the former with respect and the latter as "not entitled to consideration if they become obstinate." Typically this is the boy or man who, often with a friend or two, cruises around on Saturday night looking for a likely female. They assume that if a girl is willing to be picked up she is not sexually "innocent" and has no right to resist a sexual advance. Gang rapes often take place under these circumstances.

Still another form of sexual aggression may be homosexual. It is especially prevalent in prisons. According to an investigation conducted by the district attorney's office and the police department in Philadelphia, homosexual rape was common in the Philadelphia jails.[24] Penologists say the conditions described in Philadelphia are typical of jails and prisons through-

---

[23] A total of 13 women were so attacked and slain in the Boston area in 1962-63. Albert DeSalvo, apprehended as the mysterious strangler, confessed to the crimes and boasted of having sexually assaulted hundreds of women. He was sent to a state mental hospital and never stood trial for the crimes. See Gerald Frank, *The Boston Strangler* (1966).

[24] See Allen J. Davis, *Report on Sexual Assaults in the Philadelphia Prison System and Sheriff's Vans* (1968). See also "Racial Tensions in Prisons," *E.R.R.*, 1971 Vol. II, p. 809.

out the country. It is widely believed that homosexual attacks have less to do with sexual gratification than with status. Forcing a new inmate to submit to a homosexual advance is regarded as the ultimate prison humiliation for the victim and the ultimate achievement for the aggressor.

"Homosexual rape in prisons is particularly a problem for middle-class youths, often arrested on drug charges, naive to the system, who are less inclined to fight back because of their previous life style than are inmates of lower-class and ghetto backgrounds," said Dr. Loren H. Roth, a clinical psychiatrist at Massachusetts General Hospital who formerly was medical officer at the Lewisburg (Pa.) federal penitentiary. Writing in the January 1972 issue of *Sexual Behavior* magazine, he added: "These youths are also more articulate...than were inmates formerly, so the problem of homosexuality in prisons is now receiving more public scrutiny."

Legal Dealings With Sexual Offenses

WHEN A WOMAN brings a charge of rape against a man, whether known or unknown to her, she must first "make her case" before the police. The police investigation may be the most crucial step in determining the outcome. The police are instructed to maintain a careful balance between sympathy and skepticism when listening to her story. She will be expected to relinquish all clothing worn at the time of the attack for study of evidence. Both her physical and mental state will be closely observed.

"A rape victim must be induced to undergo medical attention," states a training paper for police on rape investigation. "This examination and treatment is not only needed for therapeutic and prophylactic reasons but it is also virtually necessary to establish proof that penetration and, therefore, rape occurred." Although the woman will probably prefer to be examined by her personal physician, this should be discouraged. "Gentle persuasion and tact will usually influence an unwilling victim or her parents to allow a physician from a public institution to conduct the examination," the document states.

The victim must be interviewed by the police for the record. "Your approach should be informal and natural in order to put the victim at ease," the police are advised. "Use words that are appropriate to the victim's age, intelligence and social class...use medical terms to refer to the various portions of the body....This portion of the investigation may well cause embarrassment...[causing the victim to] become more inhibited....You must learn to control your sentiments, remain emotionally detached but not indifferent or calloused towards the victim."[25]

Pivotal Question of Woman's 'Innocence'

In determining the validity of the woman's complaint, the police generally consider a number of factors. Of most importance is her physical and mental condition at the time first seen. If she is obviously in severe emotional distress, sobbing uncontrollably or shocked and ashamed, and if her body and clothing give evidence of violence, she is likely to be believed. Promptness in coming to the police may be a factor. While it is recognized that some women might need time to muster the nerve to bring the matter to the police, a lapse of time before doing so may give cause to suspect an ulterior motive for bringing the charge. The police apparently have had experience with women who bring weeks-old rape charges to get back at two-timing companions and with wives who get panicky when they think they have become pregnant during a husband's absence.

Another factor of importance is the relationship between the alleged rapist and the victim. If the man is a friend or dating partner, her complaint is likely to be received with some skepticism.[26] In training, the police are advised to "tactfully inquire if she has ever had sexual relations with him before." If the woman has been drinking or had gone off willingly with a man she met at a bar, the police may need considerable convincing that she was not a compliant partner. If she has made previous unfounded charges of rape, her complaint will be treated with great doubt.

The question of the sexual "innocence" of the woman technically has no standing in law. That is, rape is rape even if a woman has had sexual intercourse willingly on other occasions. But as a practical matter in the courtroom drama, juries are easily influenced to believe that a sexually "free" woman is

---

[25] International Association of Chiefs of Police, *Training Key # 128: Rape Investigation* (1969).

[26] Studies of a national sample of convicted sex offenders, drawn from police records of 17 cities and prepared for the National Commission on the Causes and Prevention of Violence, showed that rapist and victim were strangers in 53 per cent of the cases; they were members of the same family in 10 per cent.

more likely to have assented to intercourse on the occasion in question than an unmarried virgin or a chaste housewife. It becomes a factor in making a judgment on the credibility of the complainant. The woman who brings a rape charge that reaches the court may therefore expect to be questioned on her personal morals by the defense attorney.

Death, Imprisonment and Treatment for Rapists

The gravity with which society has always regarded the crime of rape is indicated by the severity of the penalties. Blinding, castration and death were among the penalties for rape in early times. "De-sexing was introduced into England, primarily as a punitive measure for rapists, by the Normans." Such laws once existed in the United States but "as early as 1872....the Eighth Amendment's 'cruel and unusual punishment' clause was held to have been enacted to prohibit, among other practices, castration."[27] Eleven states, all in the South, still retain the death penalty as the maximum punishment for forcible rape. The death penalty may be applied for statutory rape in several states if the girl is quite young—under 12 or 14. Several convicted rapists are among 694 persons who have been sentenced to death and are awaiting a Supreme Court determination on whether capital punishment is constitutional. The Court heard oral arguments on the issue Jan. 17, 1972.

Of the four test cases chosen by the Court for arguments, three dealt with rape convictions—all three involving Negro defendants and white victims. The cases were those of Earnest James Aikens Jr., convicted of raping and killing two women in Ventura, Calif.; Lucious Jackson Jr., convicted in Georgia of a brutal rape, and Elmer Branch, convicted of raping but not seriously injuring an elderly woman near Vernon, Texas. The fourth case was that of William Henry Furman, convicted of killing a man during a burglary in Chatham County, Ga.

In practice, the penalties for rape are unevenly imposed in terms of length of sentence and in application for parole or probation. Many rapists are legally juveniles. Some cases come under youth correction systems which have lenient release policies. The federal Youth Corrections Act, enacted in 1950, is currently a subject of heated courthouse debate in the District of Columbia because it is said to permit the release of young offenders, guilty of crimes of violence including

[27] David W. Meyers, *The Human Body and the Law* (1970), p. 29. Meyers reported that of 26 states which today permit human sterilization, 12 specifically include criminals. California and Washington authorize sterilization as a penalty for the crime of carnal abuse involving a girl under 10 years of age.

rape, within a few months even if they have been sentenced to many years in prison. The courts may decide, on the basis of a pre-sentencing study, to release an offender aged 18-21 on parole or send him to a rehabilitation center. Corrections officials at the center may release him on parole at any time.

Black Americans have long complained that the penalties for rape have been unevenly applied, to their disadvantage. Of the 455 men executed for rape between 1930 and 1968, 405 (89 per cent) were Negroes. Feelings on this question run deep and are still affected by memories of the era of lynching; approximately 1,200 persons accused of rape—nearly all Negroes—were lynched between 1872 and 1951. Blacks notice another insulting inequity: "Negro prisoners committed for intraracial rape get short sentences more often than whites committed for this offense....If the Negro...rapes a white woman, his penalty is heavier than that given whites who appear in court under the same circumstances."[28]

More than half of the states have enacted so-called sex psychopath laws.[29] These laws are based on the belief that certain individuals become habitual sex offenders because of some mental quirk or disorder. "The forces which prompted enactment of criminal sexual psychopath statutes were public rage and fear following highly publicized, brutal sex crimes and the reasoned demands of lawyers and psychiatrists for remedial treatment of the sex offender."[30] In general these laws provide for commitment of the offender to a treatment facility if an examination indicates he can be treated for the condition responsible for his criminal behavior. In some states the commitment procedure precedes and may replace prosecution; in others the examination may not take place until and unless he is convicted. In some states the treatment period may be indefinite and release is dependent on recovery; in several states the treatment period may not exceed the maximum prison term.

In cases where the victim cannot bring herself to undergo the emotional strain of testifying in court, there is support for conducting a pre-trial examination to determine whether a defendant meets the statutory definition of a psychopath and for his subsequent commitment if the test proves positive. This is seen as a means of protecting the community from a rapist or child molester. But civil libertarians believe this procedure

---

[28] MacDonald, *op cit.*, p. 300.

[29] Michigan adopted the first sex psychopath law in 1935 but it was declared unconstitutional. A 1938 Illinois statute was the first that was sustained.

[30] "Indiana's Sexual Psychopath Statute," *Indiana Law Journal*, Winter 1969, p. 249.

is insufficiently protective of the defendant's rights and may offer the prosecution a way out when it has a weak case. The Illinois statute, which permits pre-trial commitment of a "sexually dangerous person" without regard to his treatability, was criticized in a law journal as an "unreasonable deprivation of the individual's liberty."[31] Generally, sex psychopath laws are invoked "only when the suspect has a prior conviction for a sex-related offense...[and] when it is evident that the defendant has engaged in a pattern of sexual misconduct of a deviant nature and has not been prosecuted because of reluctance of the persons concerned to press charges."[32]

Expectation of cure in the cases of a mentally ill or compulsive sexual aggressor does not appear to be bright. "Despite the enactment of 'sex psycopath' laws...there is little evidence that sex offenders received an especially effective therapy in our penal institutions," writes Donal E. J. MacNamara, a criminologist.[33] The Violence Commission's staff study observed that therapy often comes too late because experiences during the growth period have already set the pattern of behavior. Sex psychopath laws are widely criticized as futile, especially in preventing rape. Psychiatrists do not recognize the term "sexual psychopath" as a valid medical designation.

The Kinsey study found that the sex psychopath procedure was invoked more for minor than serious sex offenses. "If the primary function of these laws is to segregate the dangerous, their objective is not being achieved, for some of the most dangerous men are those rejected as sexual psychopaths merely because they are not amenable to treatment, while some of the least dangerous...are retained."[34]

Varied Advice to Women for Their Self-Defense

In view of the pessimistic outlook on the reform of rapists, prevention of rape may be up to the women themselves. Police have issued the expected cautionary advice to women: don't walk alone on dark streets, lock your automobile door, be wary of harmless-looking but unknown "repair men" or "sales-

---

[31] "If the state fails in its burden of proof, the criminal must go free," the author argued. "There is no rational reason to treat the sex offender any differently."— Lawrence T. Burick, "An Analysis of the Illinois Sexually Dangerous Persons Act," *The Journal of Criminal Law, Criminology, and Police Science,* June 1968, p. 261.

[32] Frank W. Miller, *The Decision to Charge a Suspect With a Crime* (report of the American Bar Foundation Survey of the Administration of Criminal Justice in the United States, 1969), p. 222.

[33] Donal E. J. MacNamara (past president of American Society of Criminology), "Sex Offenses and Sex Offenders," *Annals of the American Academy of Political and Social Science,* March 1968, p. 154.

[34] Gebhard, *op. cit.,* p. 866.

men" who seek entry to your home. The police advise women not to fight back if attacked because it may incite the attacker to more violence. But women are also told that failure to resist will make prosecution very difficult. Some women are taking up karate or are defying laws against carrying concealed weapons.

There is little conflict of advice, however, on a number of basic precautions. A woman living alone, or two girls sharing an apartment, should not broadcast the fact, New York City Policewoman Betty Lee has advised. "In the lobby directory, rather than listing Miss Mary Smith, only her first initial should be used so that someone going through the lobby can't pick out what apartment is occupied by women only."

In an interview published in *Sexual Behavior* of January 1972, the policewoman added that caution should be taken in answering the door. "If it happens to be late she should give the impression that there's a man in the apartment. For instance, when she hears a knock on the door, she should say, 'John, will you answer the door?' When she gets about 15 feet from it, she can say, 'Never mind, I'll get it myself.' " Women who think they are being followed are advised not to go directly home—if no adult male is there—but to seek help from anyone who can provide it. "I think that the tide of apathy or fear is turning," the policewoman said. "Many of the women I've spoken to said that people have come forward. It's a funny thing, all you need is one person to help and then everyone else does."

Rape has become a major issue with the women's liberation movement—perhaps its first issue on which all women can unite. Women's groups in a number of cities are demanding more police patrols and brighter lights in rape-prone areas, more sensitive police treatment of women bringing rape charges, courtroom priority for rape cases, and self-defense education for girls in the schools and women in adult-education classes. Such measures may be no solution for a crime that lies deep in the sickness of society or in the twisted mind of a psychological misfit. But for the time being they will have to do.

WOMEN VOTERS

by

Mary Costello

WOMEN AND POLITICS IN 1972 ELECTION
Political Impact of Women's Liberation Movement
Women's Evaluations of Presidential Candidates
Increased Representation at Party Conventions
Women Candidates and Their Campaign Views
Public Attitudes Toward Women's Participation

CAMPAIGN FOR AND RESULTS OF SUFFRAGE
Early Suffragists and Battle for Voting Franchise
20th Century Campaigns For and Against Suffrage
Feminist Disappointment After Franchise Victory
Women's Preferences in Past Presidential Elections

WOMEN AS A GROWING POLITICAL FORCE
Outlook for Women's Movement in the Seventies
Question About Prospect of Women's Bloc Voting
Relationship of Education to an Interest in Politics

1 9 7 2
Oct. 11

WOMEN VOTERS

THE 1972 PRESIDENTIAL election will be the 14th in which American women have voted. The old anti-suffrage cliches—that when women first voted in 1920 they helped elect Warren G. Harding, a handsome but inept President, that the ladies are unable to grasp the deeper political issues and vote frivolously, if at all, or else mark their ballots as their husbands or fathers instruct—are seldom heard and rarely applauded. This year increased numbers of women have girded for political action, demanded a voice in party platforms, campaigned for candidates who support their programs, and run for office themselves.

The politicization of women is one consequence of the women's liberation movement. More than a year ago, Betty Friedan, founder of the National Organization for Women (Now), warned: "The women's liberation movement has crested now. If it doesn't become political, it will peter out, turn against itself and become nothing."[1] To gain social and economic equality, it is felt, women have to control some of the levers of power. There are now few feminine hands on these levers. Women comprise 52 per cent of the voting-age population but less than 3 per cent of all elected officials. Of the 535 members of Congress, only one elected senator [2] and 12 representatives are women. And women account for only about 315 of the more than 7,500 state legislators.[3] There are no women governors, and the National League of Cities counts only 23 women mayors.

In an attempt to remedy this situation, more than 300 women met in Washington on July 10-11, 1971, to form the National Women's Political Caucus (NWPC). Among the organizers were Ms. Friedan, writer Gloria Steinem, Rep. Shirley Chisholm (D N.Y.), the first black woman ever elected

---

[1] Quoted in *U.S. News & World Report*, Aug. 16, 1971, p. 67.
[2] Sen. Margaret Chase Smith (R Maine). Another woman serving in the Senate, Mrs. Edwin Edwards, wife of the governor of Louisiana, was appointed by her husband, Aug. 1, 1972, to fill the unexpired term of the late Allen J. Ellender (D La.).
[3] Figures used by Anne Armstrong, co-chairman of the Republican National Committee and director of its Women's Division, in a speech before the Townhall Club of Corpus Christi, Texas, Jan. 17, 1972.

to Congress, and Rep. Bella S. Abzug (D N.Y.). Participants complained that the vast majority of women in politics were regulated to behind-the-scenes dirty work—holding teas, addressing envelopes, mimeographing flyers and ringing door-bells—to help elect male candidates. The NWPC welcomed women from all political parties and agreed to help "those candidates for public or party office, whether male or female, who support women's issues and employ women in decision-making positions on their administrative and campaign staffs." The organization has formed branches at the state and local level with the ultimate goal of seeing women elected or ap-pointed to at least half of all government positions. Rep. Abzug told the Washington meeting: "Women now hold a total of 1.6 per cent of the top jobs in government...1.6 per cent is close to invisibility."

The Caucus claims 50,000 to 100,000 members. Because they tend to be relatively young, urban and surburban, well-edu-cated, middle-income women, some observers have questioned the organization's ability to influence the voting behavior of the majority of American women. However, a poll undertaken by Louis Harris for Virginia Slims cigarettes in late 1971 in-dicated that women generally are becoming more active and independent politically.[4] Evaluating the 176-page *1972 Virginia Slims American Women's Opinion Poll*, Harris wrote: "Women have sprung loose as an independent political force. They are voting differently from men.... And once you let a force like that loose, it can never be bottled up again."

Women's Evaluations of Presidential Candidates

After interviewing many of the presidential candidates in early 1972, the Women's Political Caucus released an evalua-tion of them. Not surprisingly, Shirley Chisholm was given the highest ratings. Her views, the organization stated, "are totally compatible with the Caucus's aims." Sen. George McGovern (D S.D.), the future Democratic presidential nominee, was praised as "the only male candidate who is consistently push-ing women's issues as part of his campaign and who has at-tempted to focus national attention on heretofore unpubli-cized aspects of discrimination against women.... He stated he would appoint women to his cabinet and key government positions." Richard M. Nixon, among others, did not respond to requests for position statements. The Caucus described their

---

[4] The survey consisted of interviews with 3,000 women and 1,000 men. Fifty-six per cent of the women and 51 per cent of the men agreed that the country "would be better off if women had more to say about politics"; majorities of both sexes favored new organizations to strengthen women's political participation.

silence as "persuasive evidence of a lack of commitment to women's issues."[5]

Another evaluation, based on questionnaires, interviews, public statements and voting records, was published in the spring 1972 issue of the feminist magazine *Ms*. Again Shirley Chisholm emerged as the feminist favorite. "Shirley Chisholm cares more and fights harder for women's issues than any other candidate.... She has supported every piece of legislation designed to achieve full equality for women." McGovern was praised for his promises to appoint women to high government posts and his support for the Equal Rights Amendment and liberal child-care and abortion legislation. *Ms* pointed out that 40 per cent of McGovern's national campaign staff was then composed of women. President Nixon elicited the magazine's unqualified disapproval. "Richard Nixon is neither a ladies' man nor a women's rights advocate. He seems to be nowhere when it comes to women.... Nixon's attitude toward the National Women's Political Caucus was one of ridicule."[6]

Candidate evaluations by the Caucus and the feminist *Ms* do not necessarily reflect the opinion of the majority of American women. A publication endorsed by the League of Women Voters, *You and Election '72*, said of the Caucus: "The women who have been most active have been, generally speaking, liberal, even radical, anti-war and anti-Nixon. This does not mean that they will automatically support the Democrats; but if the Caucus and the movement it represents has any success, it is more likely to help Democrats than Republicans." However, Nixon's big lead over McGovern in pre-election polling seemed to result from the woman's preference as much as from the man's. "Consistently, Richard Nixon has been weaker among women than among men, but now the two sexes are giving the incumbent President an identical 63-29 lead," Louis Harris said in releasing the results of polling conducted by his organization on Aug. 30 and Sept. 1, 1972. "His gains among women have been dramatic." A Gallup Poll taken Sept. 22-25 indicated that women were actually stronger in their support of Nixon over McGovern (64 to 30 per cent) than men were (58 to 36 per cent).

---

[5] These included Sen. Henry M. Jackson (D Wash.), Sen. Vance Hartke (D Ind.), Rep. John M. Ashbrook (R Ohio), Alabama Gov. George C. Wallace and Los Angeles Mayor Sam Yorty.

[6] It was reported that at a meeting in San Clemente, Calif., on July 13, 1971, Secretary of State William P. Rogers compared the NWPC to "a burlesque" and that the President replied: "What's wrong with that?" Referring to this episode, Bella Abzug retorted: "Obviously the President and his advisers are accustomed to viewing women only in terms of flesh shows."

Nixon and McGovern both have courted the woman's vote. McGovern has promised to appoint women to the Supreme Court and cabinet. Nixon has boasted that his administration "has appointed and promoted more women to full-time policy-making positions in the federal government than ever before." A press release issued by the White House on April 28, 1972, went on to state: "The number of women placed in policy-making positions paying $28,000 and up has nearly tripled since April 1971—from 36 to 105. More than half of these hold positions previously held only by men. We reached another milestone with the employment and/or advancement of more than 1,000 women in middle-management positions during the past year. This is particularly noteworthy because it occurred during a time when budget policy required a 5 per cent reduction in the federal work force."

Increased Representation at Party Conventions

The Women's Political Caucus set as its top priority "the fair representation of women in the 1972 national party conventions. In pursuit of this aim, the Caucus sent detailed instructions and information to each of its state branches, requesting that they seek and publish commitments from state and local party leaders on delegation makeup, and hold informational meetings for all interested women at each stage of the delegate selection process. The League of Women Voters cooperated in this project, known as Women's Education for Delegate Selection (WEDS). While neither the Democrats nor the Republicans met all of the Caucus demands, both parties increased the number of women delegates.

The women's quest for representation at the Democratic National Convention was greatly aided by reform procedures adopted after the 1968 convention at McGovern's urging. The new rules specified that state delegations must include a "reasonable representation" of women, youths and members of minority groups. Democratic officials informed state party organizations that the delegations would face a credentials challenge if the women's representation fell below 50 per cent. A number of delegations were challenged for under-representation and in several instances the Credentials Committee ruled that more women should be included.[7] When the challenges were decided, women accounted for 40 per cent of the 3,085 delegates, compared with only 13 per cent in 1968. Forty-six per cent of the McGovern delegates were women.

---

[7] See Congressional Quarterly *Weekly Report,* July 8, 1972, p. 1640.

Republicans also made efforts, though less dramatic and less publicized than the Democrats, to increase the number and visibility of women delegates when the party held its National Convention on Aug. 21-23 in Miami Beach, where the Democratic Party had convened July 10-13. Women made up 30 per cent of the entire Republican delegation, in contrast to 17 per cent four years earlier. "This is the year of the woman," declared Barbara Franklin, a staff assistant to President Nixon, at a meeting of the Women's Political Caucus in Miami Beach on the eve of the Republican convention. A similar sense of euphoria attended the opening of the Democratic convention. It represented, according to author-feminist Germaine Greer, "the first emergence of women as a significant group in electoral politics."

But euphoria soon turned to bitterness. Ms. Greer charged in an account of the convention she wrote for the October 1972 issue of *Harper's* magazine that the women were too willing to scuttle a strong pro-abortion plank for fear it would hurt McGovern in the election campaign. Similar complaints were voiced after the Republican convention. Shana Alexander wrote that at both conventions the abortion issue "stayed buried with the active connivance of the very women charged by their sisters with responsibility for bringing it to the floor." These "front-women—Shirley MacLaine for the Democrats and Jill Ruckelshaus for the Republicans—each sold her sex down the river in the name of political expediency."[8]

Women Candidates and Their Campaign Views

On other issues, women's groups fared better. In both platforms, the parties supported the Equal Rights Amendment pending in state legislatures, backed legislation to expand the jurisdiction of the U.S. Civil Rights Commission to include discrimination against women, and pledged support for child-care programs—although the Republican pledge was qualified, in deference to President Nixon's veto of a child-care bill in December 1971.[9] At the Democratic convention, Rep. Chisholm received 151 votes for the presidential nomination. **Frances Farenthold, recently defeated for governor of Texas after a strong showing,** received 408 votes for the vice presidential nomination—second only to Sen. Thomas F. Eagleton of Missouri.

---

[8] Shana Alexander, "The Politics of Abortion," *Newsweek*, Oct. 2, 1972, p. 29. Shirley MacLaine, the movie actress, was a Democratic delegate from California. Mrs. Ruckelshaus, wife of William D. Ruckelshaus, administrator of the federal Environmental Protection Agency, represented the Caucus at the Republican convention.

[9] See "Child Care," *E.R.R.*, 1972 Vol. I, pp. 447-449.

The only other woman gubernatorial candidate in the 1972 primary elections, Eva Levengood Shunkwiler, a Montana Democrat, also lost. And only two of the 10 women senatorial candidates in the primaries survived. They were Sen. Margaret Chase Smith (R Maine), and Louise Leonard, a West Virginia Republican. Of the 76 women counted in House races, 35 went on to face general election opponents Nov. 7. The victorious candidates included Elizabeth Holtzman, a 31-year-old Brooklyn lawyer, who unseated Rep. Emanuel Celler (D N.Y.), 84-year-old dean of the House and chairman of its Judiciary Committee. Rep. Abzug lost in the same New York Democratic primary on June 20 but later was awarded the party's nomination upon the death of her foe, Rep. William F. Ryan. In the general election, she faces four candidates—three of them women—including Ryan's widow.

Minor party candidates and late entries, such as Mrs. Ryan and Helen Meyner, the wife of a former New Jersey governor, who replaced a candidate after the primary election, increased the total number of women candidates for the House in November 1972 to at least 59. Two years earlier, in contrast, 38 women sought election to the House. Of these, 12 were successful.[10] Lenore Romney, the only woman Senate candidate in 1970, was unable to unseat Sen. Philip A. Hart (D Mich.)

Anne Armstrong has said "the big surge for women in public office is at the local level; it is still unrealistic to think that a woman can pull out stakes and move to the state capital or Washington." [11] Two women, however, appeared more than willing to pull up stakes and move to the White House. Congresswomen Shirley Chisholm and Patsy T. Mink (D Hawaii) were announced presidential candidates. Rep. Chisholm, who campaigned in a number of primary contests, often complained that she had encountered more discrimination as a woman than as a black. In announcing her intention to seek the presidency on Jan. 25, 1972, she said: "I stand before you today to repudiate the ridiculous notion that the American people will not vote for a qualified candidate simply because he is not white or because she is not a male. I do not believe that, in 1972, the great majority of Americans will continue to harbor such narrow and petty prejudices."[12]

---

[10] Charlotte T. Reid (R Ill.) resigned in July 1971 to take a seat on the Federal Communications Commission and was replaced by a man. Elizabeth Andrews (D Ala.) was elected on April 4, 1972, to fill the vacancy caused by the death of her husband, George W. Andrews. This left the total number of congresswomen unchanged at 12.

[11] See Congressional Quarterly *Weekly Report,* April 22, 1972, p. 883.

[12] Shirley Chisholm is not the first black woman to seek the presidency. Charlene Mitchell of New York was the Communist Party's presidential candidate in 1968.

Nevertheless a number of Americans, both male and female, seem to feel that a woman is physiologically and emotionally unsuited for the nation's top office. At a meeting of the Democratic Party's Committee on National Priorities in April 1970, Dr. Edgar Berman, Sen. Hubert Humphrey's physician and adviser, said that because of hormonal changes during menstruation, pregnancy and menopause, women might be "subject to...curious mental aberrations...." Rep. Mink, demanding Berman's ouster from the committee, retorted: "His use of the menstrual cycle and menopause to ridicule women and to caricature all women as neurotic and emotionally unbalanced was as indefensible and astonishing as those who still believe, let alone dare state, that the Negro is physiologically inferior." A number of eminent doctors disputed Berman's thesis and, under pressure, he resigned his advisory post.

Public Attitudes Toward Women's Participation

Surveys indicate that the number of voters who would support a woman candidate for President is increasing. A Gallup Poll, released on Aug. 5, 1971, showed that 66 per cent of those questioned—65 per cent of the men and 67 per cent of the women—would vote for a qualified woman presidential candidate. A similar study in March 1969 indicated that 54 per cent—58 per cent of the men and only 49 per cent of the women—were then willing to do so. In 1937, a mere 31 per cent of the voters questioned said they would support a woman presidential candidate. The Harris-Virginia Slims poll in 1972 recorded that 40 per cent of the women said they would be less likely to vote for a woman than for an equally qualified male candidate. However, 57 per cent of the women and 58 per cent of the men felt that the country would be ready to elect a woman President in the next 20 years.

The same survey indicated that three out of four women felt that women in public office could be as logicial and rational as men. Despite the fact that both men and women seen to be losing their prejudice against women candidates, the actual number of women holding elective office in the country has not increased—and in some cases has actually decreased—in the last 10 years. Today there are only 14 women in Congress; 10 years ago there were 19. According to the Washington, D.C., branch of the Women's Political Caucus, there were 346 women in state legislatures in 1960 but only 315 in 1971.

Women have never constituted a separate voting bloc in the sense that labor or black people have. There is nothing to indicate that the majority of American women will vote exclusively for female candidates or for male candidates sympathetic to women's issues. Yet groups like the Women's Political Caucus may have politicized enough women to make a difference in some elections. Gloria Steinem contends: "Even a small difference can be crucial.... It may only take a few thousand people in each state to change an election.... We've been voting differently for quite a long time, but we've been delivering our votes for nothing. Now, women want something in return. 1972 is just the beginning."[13]

In only three countries of the world have women reached the pinnacle of elective political power. These women are Prime Ministers Indira Gandhi of India, Golda Meir of Israel and Sirimavo Bandaranaike of Ceylon.[14] But the tide of history appears to be running strong against the disenfranchisement of women. Only six countries still refuse women the vote solely because of their sex. They are Jordan, Kuwait, Liechtenstein, Nigeria, Saudi Arabia and the Yemen Arab Republic. Switzerland voted in 1971 to let women cast ballots in federal elections and they promptly won 11 seats in the national legislature. However, Swiss women are still barred from local elections in a few rural German-speaking cantons.

Campaign For and Results of Suffrage

WOMEN'S SUFFRAGE was not a popular issue in 19th century America. William J. O'Neill noted: "It is hard for us now to appreciate the strength and courage of the early feminists who set themselves against a network of ideas, prejudices, and almost religious emotionalism that simultaneously degraded and elevated women."[15] The pioneer feminists of the early 19th century began what then seemed an almost hopeless battle against an entrenched way of life, solidified by law, moral conviction and religion, which kept women and especially married women in the status of chattels or at best dependent children. The early movement was by no means confined to a struggle for suffrage. More immediate concerns

---

[13] "Women Voters Can't be Trusted," *Ms*, July 1972, p. 131.

[14] Mrs. Gandhi and Mrs. Bandaranaike have won election twice—the second time by large majorities. All three are generally considered by friends and foes to be consummate and pragmatic politicians, able to weld together opposing factions and diverse points of view.

[15] William J. O'Neill, *Everyone Was Brave* (1969), p. 7.

were control of property, of earnings, guardianship, divorce, opportunity for education and employment, lack of legal status, and the concept of female inferiority perpetuated by established religion.

Early Suffragists and Battle for Voting Franchise

The Woman's Rights Convention at Seneca Falls, N.Y., in July 1848, is generally cited as the beginning of the women's suffrage movement in the United States. But the Declaration of Principles which Elizabeth Cady Stanton read at that meeting and which thereafter became a sacred text for the movement, was a much broader and more revolutionary document than a simple claim for the franchise. Paraphrasing the Declaration of Independence, it held "these truths to be self-evident; that all men and women are created equal." It itemized women's grievances—"a history of repeated injuries and usurpations on the part of men toward women"—and pledged an unremitting fight, in the face of anticipated punishment from society, to attain the goal of equality. The meeting adopted a number of resolutions, unanimously except for one—a call for women's suffrage, which carried by a small margin.

Early crusaders for women's rights were often active in the anti-slavery movement. "It was in the abolition movement that women first learned to organize, to hold public meetings, to conduct petition campaigns. As abolitionists they first won the right to speak in public, and they began to evolve a philosophy of their own place in society and of their basic rights. For a quarter of a century, the two movements, to free the slave and liberate the woman, nourished and strengthened one another."[16] The women who had worked for the freedom and enfranchisement of the Negro were bitterly disappointed when the 15th Amendment to the Constitution gave black men but not women—white or black—the right to vote. The humiliation felt by middle- and upper-class suffragettes led many of them to exploit the prejudices against both blacks and the foreign-born. They appealed for a restricted franchise which would give middle-class women the vote but would deny it to the despised classes. The suffrage movement dropped this bid for support after 1910, but it left among lower-class men and women a residue of hostility toward the women's rights movement.

In an attempt to rally the discouraged suffragettes, two organizations—the National Woman Suffrage Association and

---

[16] Eleanor Flexner, *"Century of Struggle: The Women's Rights Movement in the United States* (1959), p. 41.

the American Woman Suffrage Association—were formed in 1869. The former, headed by Elizabeth Cady Stanton and Susan B. Anthony, worked for a constitutional amendment to enfranchise women while the latter, led by Lucy Stone and Julia Ward Howe, gave priority to a state-by-state approach. After 1870, both groups tended to reject the more radical appeals for full equality for women and to concentrate on the suffrage issue. The two organizations came together as the National American Woman Suffrage Association in 1890. United or separate, neither had much tangible success in the 19th century. By 1900, only four underpopulated states— Wyoming, Colorado, Utah and Idaho—had granted women the franchise. A constitutional amendment was introduced in Congress in 1878, but did not come to a vote until 1887 and then was defeated by the Senate.

20th Century Campaigns For and Against Suffrage

In the two decades preceding women's enfranchisement, extravagant claims were made by extremists on both sides. Radical feminists often insisted that women voters would be able to cleanse American politics of its corruption and usher in some ill-defined, utopian golden age. Anti-franchise forces were no less impractical in their claims. During World War I, Henry A. Wise Wood, president of the Aero Club of America, told the House Committee on Woman Suffrage that giving women the vote would mean "the dilution with the qualities of the cow, of the qualities of the bull upon which all the herd's safety must depend."[17] And the January 1917 issue of *Remonstrance,* an anti-suffrage journal, cautioned that women's suffrage would lead to the nationalization of women, free love and communism.

Both sides had cogent arguments for their positions. Pro-suffrage advocates, basing their case on the 1848 Declaration of Principles proposition that all men *and women* are created equal, contended that it was indefensible for democratic America to deny half of its citizens the right to vote. The more pragmatic anti-suffragists pointed out that in states where women were allowed to vote, the effect on politics was slight. Federal Judge Moses Hallett remarked that in Colorado "the presence of women at the polls has only augmented the total votes; it has worked no radical changes. It has produced no special reforms, and it has had no particularly purifying effect upon politics."[18]

---

[17] Quoted by O'Neill, *op. cit.,* p. 56.
[18] *Ibid.,* p. 64.

"The friends of the suffrage movement in America were a mixed lot: in the West popularism and the frontier spirit; in the Middle West, temperance; in the East, reform," Kate Millett wrote in her 1970 best seller, *Sexual Politics.* "The enemies of the suffrage movement were also an interesting group: southern racists fearful of the votes of black women, middle western liquor interests, eastern capitalism, and machine politics. In the last two there was considerable, finally largely unjustified, anxiety that women might play a strong role in unionization and political reform. Corporations opposed the vote for women and, like the liquor trust, stood willing to finance anti-suffrage campaigns; both were rash enough to leave the evidence behind." The opposition also included a large number of women, many of whom joined the National Association Opposed to Women Suffrage.

The campaigns for and against enfranchisement intensified during the second decade of the 20th century. After a 14-year hiatus, the state of Washington granted women the vote in 1910. California followed in 1911 and Kansas, Oregon, Arizona, Montana and Nevada in 1914. The growing support for woman suffrage led both major political parties to include planks in their 1916 platform approving it in principle and advocating a state-by-state rather than a federal-amendment approach. That same year, the first woman—Jeannette Rankin, a Montana Republican—was elected to Congress and the National American Woman Suffrage Association, led by Carrie Chapman Catt, decided to concentrate on a constitutional amendment rather than individual state enfranchisement to gain the vote.

About this time, a split between the more militant and conservative suffragists became more pronounced. The former, led by Woman's Party founder Alice Paul, turned to picketing when their lobbying efforts failed to convince more congressmen to support the amendment. When the United States entered World War I in April 1917, Miss Paul decided to continue the picketing and ignore the war effort. In contrast, Mrs. Catt and other NAWSA leaders felt that women had to take an active part in war work in order not to antagonize the forces that would be needed for the suffrage movement to succeed. They consequently disavowed many of the actions of the Woman's Party.

The most publicized of the Woman's Party picketing began on Jan. 10, 1917. The following June pickets were arrested for "obstructing traffic." During the summer, a number of women, including Alice Paul, were imprisoned. The publicity engendered by the arrests and the harsh treatment given the suffragettes in jail proved both annoying and embarrassing to President Wilson. Janice Law Trecher, writing in the summer 1972 issue of *American Scholar,* contended: "The brutality the suffragettes encountered, in both the District [of Columbia] Jail and the Occoquan [Va.] Workhouse, was not simply the result of their feminist agitation. The prison officials, the District administration, and ultimately the Wilson government attempted to crush them because they raised basic issues of civil liberties and personal freedom, issues that were considered dangerous in wartime."

When suffrage was finally won in 1920, both the NAWSA and the Woman's Party took full credit for the victory. Mrs. Catt asserted that Alice Paul and her followers had hindered and almost ruined women's quest for the vote. However, a chronicler of the suffrage movement has noted: "Politicians in general were soon convinced of two things. They would not yield a foot to the outrageous Woman's Party, and yet something had to be done about suffrage. Its patient, suave, conservative tactics soon put the National-American [organization] in a position to profit from these feelings. Politicians felt no loss of face in giving into them. The result was that the Woman's Party pressure did seem to produce a change. Miss Paul's adherents freely claimed all the credit, while the other suffragists denied them any. The truth seems to have been that the major part of the progress was due to the larger group, once it got started. Notwithstanding, Miss Paul's early work and the publicity earned by her pickets played a valuable part alongside the campaigns of Carrie Catt."[19]

Feminist Disappointment After Franchise Victory

President Wilson, who had already spoken in favor of a suffrage amendment, called Congress into special session in May 1919 to consider the measure. The House acted on May 21, and the Senate 14 days later,[20] to submit the 19th Amendment—which held that "the right of citizens of the United States to vote shall not be denied or abridged by the United States or by any State on account of sex"—to the states for ratification. That summer, Carrie Chapman Catt, in a speech to the National American Woman Suffrage Association's Jubilee Convention in St. Louis, proposed a non-

---

[19] Olivia Coolidge, *Women's Rights: The Suffrage Movement in America, 1848-1920* (1967), pp. 145-146.

[20] The House vote was 304 to 89 and the Senate vote was 56 to 25. See "Status of Women," *E.R.R.*, 1970 Vol. II, p. 565.

partisan League of Women Voters to educate the soon-to-be-enfranchised American woman.

On Aug. 18, 1920, Tennessee became the 36th and last state needed to ratify the amendment and on Aug. 26, the final proclamation giving women the right to vote was signed by Secretary of State Bainbridge Colby. In the years between the first introduction of the amendment in Congress in 1866 and final victory, the suffragists had conducted 480 campaigns to get legislatures to submit suffrage amendments to voters; 47 campaigns to get state constitutional conventions to write women's suffrage into state constitutions; 277 campaigns to get state party conventions to include women's suffrage planks; 30 campaigns to get national party conventions to adopt women's suffrage planks in party platforms; and 19 campaigns with 19 successive Congresses.

Was it worth the time or effort? The suffragettes had, of necessity, declared that much good would be accomplished when women were finally allowed to cast their ballots. But after 1920, the women's movement splintered and American politics was little changed. In the decade after suffrage, the crusade for women's rights fell to the Woman's Party. The WP, which never enjoyed mass female, much less male, support, embarked on a campaign for an equal rights amendment to the Constitution. Such an amendment was first introduced in Congress in 1923 and, almost 50 years later, on March 22, 1972, won approval for submission to the states for ratification.[21] Within six months, the legislatures in 20 of the required 38 states had ratified the amendment.[22] In 1970, at age 85, Alice Paul told a reporter: "This amendment turned out to be harder than suffrage. Suffrage didn't take anything away from men. But now men feel that women's equal rights will mean competition for them—so they've invented laws that they say are to protect women."[23]

Two years after women won the vote, H. L. Mencken published *In Defense of Women,* in which he contended, only half-jokingly: "Years ago I predicted that these suffragettes, tired out by victory, would turn out to be idiots. They are

---

[21] By a Senate vote of 84 to 8. The House vote, five months earlier, was 354 to 23.

[22] They were Alaska, Colorado, Delaware, Hawaii, Idaho, Iowa, Kansas, Kentucky, Maryland, Massachusetts, Michigan, Nebraska, New Hampshire, New Jersey, New York, Rhode Island, South Dakota, Texas, West Virginia and Wisconsin. Opposition defeated the amendment, at least temporarily, in five other states: Illinois, Louisiana, Connecticut, Oklahoma and Vermont.

[23] Quoted by Carol H. Falk in *The Wall Street Journal,* July 31, 1970. In the same interview, Miss Paul expressed disappointment about lack of support from women for the Equal Rights Amendment. "It's strange that so few women cared very much about freedom or the status of women."

now hard at work proving it. Half of them devote themselves to advocating reforms, chiefly of a sexual character, so utterly preposterous that even male politicians and newspaper editors laugh at them; the other half succumb absurdly to the blandishments of the old-time male politicians, and so enroll themselves in the great political parties. A woman who joins one of these parties simply becomes an imitation man, which is to say, a donkey. Thereafter she is nothing but an obscure cog in an ancient and creaking machine, the sole intelligible purpose of which is to maintain a horde of scoundrels in public office."

In *Everyone Was Brave* (1969), William J. O'Neill gave a more objective appraisal of the effects of women's suffrage. "It took seventy-two years for women to get the vote. Generations wore out their lives in pursuit of it. Some women went to jail, many picketed, marched, and protested their deprived state in other ways. In the last stages of the fight for equal suffrage, literally millions of women contributed something to the cause. Yet when the vote was gained it made little difference to the feminine condition. A few women were elected to office, political campaigning became more refined, and the sex lives of candidates were more rigorously policed. The ballot did not materially help women to advance their most urgent causes; even worse, it did not help women to better themselves or improve their status. The struggle for women's rights ended during the 1920s, leaving men in clear possession of the commanding places in American life."

Women's Preferences in Past Presidential Elections

In the 1920 presidential election—the first in which women were allowed to vote—only about 30 per cent of the eligible women were believed to have cast their ballots. Analyses of the 1924 election indicated that scarcely one-third of all eligible women voted while more than two-thirds of the eligible men had done so.[24] The woman's electoral performance came as a bitter blow to the suffragists. Dr. Anna Shaw, the crusading ex-president of the NAWSA, told an interviewer after women won the vote: "I am sorry for you young women who have to carry on the work in the next ten years, for suffrage was a symbol, and now you have lost your symbol. There is nothing for women to rally around."[25]

According to Census Bureau statistics, 66 percent of the eligible women went to the polls in 1968, compared to 69.8

[24] See "Women in Politics," *E.R.R.*, 1956 Vol. I, p. 121.
[25] Quoted by William J. O'Neill, *op. cit.*, p. 268.

per cent of the men.[26] Despite the increasing number of women choosing to exercise their franchise, there is still no symbol for the vast majority of women to rally around. Gallup Poll findings recorded by Richard M. Scammon and Ben J. Wattenberg in their book, *The Real Majority* (1970), indicate that women differed from men by no more than 6 per cent in their choice of a President at any time since 1952. The high point of 6 per cent was recorded in 1956 by a strong woman's preference for Dwight D. Eisenhower over Adlai E. Stevenson in their second race, as is shown in the table on the following page. This pattern would seem to bear out an observation by the University of Michigan's Survey Research Center in its 1960 publication, *The American Voter:* "The dependence of a wife's vote on her husband's partisan predisposition appears to be the one reason why the entrance of women into the electorate has tended to make little visible difference in the partisan distribution of the national vote."

Voting statistics gathered by the Research Center for the presidential elections of 1948 through 1968 indicate that women did not gravitate to any one party or candidate. They favored a Democrat, Harry S Truman, in 1948 but voted heavily for a Republican, Eisenhower, in 1952 and 1956. In 1960, women favored Nixon over John F. Kennedy but in 1968 they favored Hubert H. Humphrey over Nixon. The 1960 election has been offered by some women's liberationists, including Gloria Steinem, as proof that women do not necessarily favor the more physically attractive candidate.

Women as a Growing Political Force

MARJORIE LANSING, associate professor of political science at Eastern Michigan University, evaluated women's voting behavior from 1948 to 1968 for a doctoral thesis, "Sex Differences in Political Participation," she wrote in 1970. She presented statistical information purporting to show that in voter participation women trailed men by at least 10 percentage points from 1948 through 1960. "The 1950s were a disastrous decade for women," she explained.

---

[26] The Census Bureau did not begin compiling voting statistics by sex until after the 1964 election. Charles Johnson, a spokesman for the Bureau, admitted that the 1968 figures may be as much as 8 percentage points too high because of over-response to census questionnaires. Gloria Steinem asserts that only 58 per cent of the eligible women voted in 1968.

PRESIDENTIAL BALLOTING BY MEN AND WOMEN

| | 1956 | | 1960 | |
	Stevenson	Eisenhower	Kennedy	Nixon
Total	42.2%	57.8%	50.1%	49.9%
Men	45	55	52	48
Women	39	61	49	51

| | 1964 | | 1968 | | |
	Johnson	Goldwater	Humphrey	Nixon	Wallace
Total	61.3%	38.7%	43.0%	43.4%	13.6%
Men	60	40	41	43	16
Women	63	38	45	43	12

"The birthrate from 1946 to 1957 increased at an almost unprecedented rate. The implications of the population boom produced adverse effects on the status of women in general. These years were accompanied by declines in the proportion of women seeking careers and graduate study, and unquestionably retarded the politicization of women."

In the next two presidential elections, the difference between male and female voter participation was down to about 3 per cent. Professor Lansing surmised that the "decline in the differential...in 1964 and 1968 reflects the gradual politicization of women." She warned that "survey findings of the 1940s and 1950s are an inadequate guide to the political behavior of women in the 1970s.... For the elections of the 1970s, female voters and female activists will differ from male groups primarily because of their link to the developing women's liberation. For the first time in 50 years we are witnessing on the American scene a woman's movement which is self-interested, coming into consciousness along with the new racial, ethnic, religious and student groups."

A comparison of women's opinion recorded in 1970 by the Harris-Virginia Slims poll with that of the following year indicates that an increasing number of women are attracted to the women's liberation movement. In the earlier survey, 42 per cent favored "efforts to strengthen and change women's status in society" while 40 per cent were opposed. A year later, 48 per cent approved of such efforts while only 36 per cent disapproved. The strongest support for status changes came from "an essentially urban bloc of single, divorced and/or separated women, black women, college educated women and women under 30."

Louis Harris, commenting on the results of the 1971 survey, concluded: "There are many signs that women are now playing for keeps in politics more than at any time in the past and that this activism will accelerate....The cause of advancing women's status has literally leaped forward among women since a year ago....Clearly these results point to a condition of growing confidence, determination, and bitterness that combine to make a potential explosion of woman-power in American politics."

Question About Prospect of Women's Bloc Voting

While women may begin to demand more support from male candidates on issues of importance to them, there is considerable doubt whether they will support women candidates in large numbers. The 1972 Harris-Virginia Slims poll found that 63 per cent of both the men and women interviewed felt that "most men are better suited emotionally for politics than are most women." There may well be more than a handful of women who agree with a statement attributed to a veteran Pennsylvania politician: "You'll always find a handful of odd-ball women who'll run for office, but while they may be right in doing it, most women are inherently passive. They're build that way physically, and their whole emotional and intellectual range doesn't suit them as a sex for the kind of long-range commitment, the wheeling and dealing, the ability to balance principle and expeditiousness that makes for a successful politician."[27]

There appears to be some contention within the women's movement itself over unqualified support for women candidates. Gloria Steinem has repeatedly assured women seeking public office that she will campaign vigorously for them if it would help, or refrain from campaigning if it would not. Betty Friedan criticized Ms. Steinem, and she objected to Rep. Abzug's race in the New York Democratic primary against Rep. William F. Ryan, who had "a long and excellent voting record on peace and women's rights."

> Only a female chauvinist would say that no matter how good a man's record—on peace, on women—women must support a female opponent just because she is a woman. That would invite men to vote *against* women simply because they are women. The essence of political power for women, as well as for men, has to be some principle of reward or support for those who fight for us and seek revenge against our enemies.[28]

Ms. Steinem denied the charges and labelled them "a personal attack." Rep. Abzug, in a statement issued in Washington, also rejected the "female chauvinist" accusation, con-

---

[27] Quoted by John Gunther, "The Political Prisoners of Sex," *Philadelphia Magazine*, July 1972, p. 156.
[28] Betty Friedan, "Beyond Women's Liberation," *McCall's*, August 1972, p. 134.

tending: "Once again Betty Friedan has exercised her right to be wrong."

In the years to come, it can be expected that as American women become better educated they will also become more involved in political issues. Marjorie Lansing notes: "Projections for education suggest increasing numbers of women graduating from high school and attending college. Education has been found in our study to affect the politicization of women more than men. Thus, predictions of a younger, better educated, and more highly employed population suggest increasing political participation by women."

The National Women's Political Caucus, preparing for the 1972 election and reflecting its strong women's liberation orientation, developed a Women's Plank, most of which was accepted by the Democratic Convention for its party platform. The 1972 Louis Harris-Virginia Slims poll indicated that women tended to be more concerned about the war in Viet Nam, drug abuse, pollution, crime, poverty, education, gun control and racial tension than men. On both hard drug use and marijuana, men were more likely to recommend prison penalties while women favored medical treatment. More than 80 per cent of the women wanted a system of strict gun control, compared with only 63 per cent of the men.

There are few indications that American women will be able to form a cohesive voting bloc or a viable political party during the 1970s. Their ideological differences remain too great; their opinions on specific issues are too diverse. What seems more likely is the formation of a number of formal and informal women's groups, based on the political proclivities of their members. The effectiveness of such groups will depend to a large extent on the alliances they form—with like-minded racial and ethnic groups, labor, youth and others. If women in large numbers decide to join these coalitions, they can be expected to devote themselves much more to the political issues than to making and serving the coffee.

LEGALIZATION OF PROSTITUTION

by

Mary Costello

GROWING PROBLEMS OF PROSTITUTION
Relation of Rising Incidence to VD, Drugs, Crime
Crackdown by New York Police on Streetwalkers
Varied Views About Prostitution; Its Practitioners
Role of Males as Pimps, Homosexuals and Gigolos
Persistence of Prostitution Despite Sex Revolution

AMERICAN PROSTITUTION AND THE LAW
Practices and Penalties Through 19th Century
Heyday of City Brothels and Red-Light Districts
Upsurge and Control of Prostitution in Wartime
Enforcement of Vice Laws Since World War II

DEBATE OVER ISSUES OF LEGALIZATION
Limited Attempts at Regulation in United States
Legalized Prostitution in Other Times and Places
Unclear Effects of Control on Disease and Crime

1 9 7 1
Aug. 25

LEGALIZATION OF PROSTITUTION

T HE WORLD'S OLDEST PROFESSION is thriving. Though reliable figures are lacking, it is estimated that 250,000 to 500,000 American women engage in prostitution on a full-time basis and that many times more work on a part-time basis. FBI Uniform Crime Reports show that the total arrests for prostitution increased 61 per cent between 1960 and 1969. For women under 18 years of age, the increase was almost 120 per cent during that time. The number of both male and female prostitutes in the United States is clearly growing. And so is public concern.

Closely connected with prostitution are the problems of venereal disease, drug addiction, and various crimes against persons and property. According to Judge Morris Schwalb of the New York City Criminal Court, "Venereal disease has reached epidemic proportions, and streetwalking prostitutes contribute to the disease in large measure."[1] As many as nine of every 10 full-time prostitutes are infected with venereal disease at some time during their careers. Drug addiction among prostitutes has soared. It is estimated that up to 50 per cent of all prostitutes in the nation's larger cities are addicted, usually to heroin. Addicted prostitutes are frequently involved in other criminal activities, especially robbery, assault and blackmail, to support their habit.

Prostitution and the problems associated with it have led some to argue that communities should make prostitution legal so that it could be supervised and controlled. Arguments for legalization are that it would bring about close medical supervision and thus lessen venereal disease and drug addiction; that it would keep prostitutes off the streets and place them in segregated districts; that it would tend to eliminate pimps and others who live off the earnings of prostitutes; that it would save the police considerable time and money; and finally that it would be a far less hypocritical way of dealing with a problem that will not go away.

[1] Quoted in *The New York Times*, July 6, 1971.

127

Adherents of these views find an unlikely supporter in Thomas Aquinas, the 13th century scholastic philosopher. He argued that prostitution was a permanent evil and should be kept in restricted areas to protect those in other places. In one form or another, similar thoughts have been voiced ever since. The San Francisco Crime Commission in June 1971 publicly asked for the repeal of most anti-prostitution laws, saying that the police should stop wasting their time prosecuting "discreet private sin" not involving violence. The League for Sexual Freedom and other groups have been actively campaigning for the legalization of prostitution.

However, the movement to legalize prostitution has not gained major support in this country. Apart from the outcries that legalization would sanction immorality and endanger the fabric of society, opponents argue that legalized prostitution would be degrading to its practitioners and impossible to control. Anthropologist Margaret Mead writes: "To me the evil thing about legalized prostitution where it exists...lies in the exploitation of women who have no other form of livelihood and in the exploitation of the desires of lonely strangers."[2]

New York Police Crackdown on Streetwalkers

The prevalence of prostitution in New York City has caused a considerable division of opinion between those wanting to legalize it and those wishing for stricter enforcement of existing laws. For the moment, at least, the latter view seems to be dominant. The city's prostitution problems became newsworthy internationally in March 1971 when three prostitutes were implicated in the stabbing death of a visiting Italian manufacturer, Pasquale Bottero, and others were questioned about the mugging-robbery of a former West German cabinet minister, Franz Josef Strauss, in a car outside the fashionable Plaza Hotel.

Streetwalking prostitutes became more and more brazen, venturing away from familiar Times Square surroundings into the rich East Side of mid-Manhattan. Arrests soared. Judge Schwalb, in outrage, refused bail for two prostitutes and ordered them jailed—the first refusal of its kind that veteran court observers in New York could remember. The next day, July 7, Mayor John V. Lindsay announced plans for a crackdown after his office was deluged with com-

---

[2] Quoted in *Redbook*, April 1971, pp. 50-51. Dr. Abraham Flexner, in his 1914 classic study, *Prostitution in Europe*, concluded that licensed prostitution could never work effectively because most prostitutes did not register with the authorities.

plaints from midtown visitors and residents. Lindsay had already made known his opposition to legalized prostitution.

"Ordinarily, police drives against prostitution are about as effective as pacification programs in Viet Nam," Gail Sheehy wrote in *New York* magazine. "Police respond to the immediate public outcry. Their 'street sweeps' last only until the courts are choked with insubstantial cases and a louder cry comes back from the district attorney's office to the police commissioner's office: lay off. Meanwhile, the girls evicted from one territory simply move to another, wait for calm, and return."[3]

Varied Views About Prostitution; Its Practitioners

It has been observed that there would be no prostitution if there were no demand for it. And it seems safe to say that as long as there is a demand there will be a ready supply of prostitutes. Public opinion about prostitution varies widely. Literature is filled with prostitutes who had hearts of gold— of fallen women waiting to be reclaimed. The prostitute has also been portrayed as a depraved creature who deserves to suffer. Opinion ranges from the contention of radical feminist Ti-Grace Atkinson that "the prostitute is the only honest woman left in America" to William Acton's assertion that she is "a social pest, carrying contamination and foulness to every quarter to which she has access."[4]

Miss Sheehy offers still another view, that of a "new breed" of prostitute whose business is not so much to dispense pleasure as to mug, swindle, and possibly even murder her patrons. "For in a crazy, incoherent form the message of women's lib has seeped through to prostitutes," she wrote. "Why give one's body into the bargain when men go about crime so much more directly? Why not attack the john, take his money and be done with it?"

Trying to make prostitutes conform to one's own thinking is a risky business. Their behavior is not easy to label and characterize. However, among prostitutes there is a pecking order. The aristocrats of the trade are call girls, or "pony girls," who are women usually in their late twenties or early thirties,

---

[3] Gail Sheehy, "The New Breed," *New York*, July 26, 1971, p. 22. Her account of prostitution has become an object of journalistic controversy. *The Wall Street Journal* reported Aug. 13, 1971, that her portrayal of a prostitute called "Redpants" was not of an actual person but a composite picture of several prostitutes—although the magazine's readers were not so informed.

[4] William Acton, *Prostitution* (1969 reprint of book originally published in 1851), p. 118.

expensively groomed, attractive and relatively sophisticated. A call girl might average seeing 60 men a month. According to an expert: "Call girls now earn in the neighborhood of thirty thousand dollars a year. Since they live outside the law, all this is untaxed. The girls charge from fifty to a hundred dollars for each session and on occasion...more. The higher figures are paid either by extremely affluent people or by those who have special tastes for which the girls want extra pay."[5]

Most call girls use a telephone answering service and keep individual dates with clients. Some have a manager who arranges meetings with customers and receives a percentage of the earnings. Call girls are found primarily in the better sections of cities and in expensive hotel districts, resorts, and convention areas. Because call girls do not openly solicit customers, they seldom come into contact with the police.

Next in the prostitute hierarchy come the house girls. Today's few remaining brothels are a far cry from their more numerous and exotic counterparts of 50 years ago. They are likely to be simple and inconspicuous, open only in the daytime—to avoid police harassment—and provide only two to four girls. Very few allow customers to stay overnight. Similar to the brothel, and becoming more popular, are massage parlors. The *Los Angeles Times* estimated on April 6, 1971, that in Los Angeles and Orange counties "there are now more than 150 of these new-style houses of prostitution...each open fifteen to twenty hours a day, six or seven days a week—and an educated estimate of their gross annual income exceeds $50 million a year." Other establishments allow customers to fingerpaint or photograph naked women in private rooms. The former manager of one of these "art" centers in New York estimated that the models earned from $350 to $500 a week. He added: "These places are the first step toward legalized prostitution."[6]

A step below the house girls are the bar and night club prostitutes. While these girls do not usually solicit men, they make no attempt to conceal their vocation and are readily available as soon as they are contacted. They usually earn far less than call girls and house prostitutes. As these girls become older and less attractive, they are often forced into streetwalking. Streetwalkers are scorned by their more prestigious sisters as well as by the people who subsidize them.

---

[5] Harold Greenwald, *The Elegant Prostitute* (1970), p. 10.

[6] Quoted in *The New York Times*, July 11, 1971.

They are generally less attractive, less educated and inevitably less well-paid than other prostitutes. Streetwalkers are found almost exclusively in large cities. Because of their flagrant way of dressing and approaching customers, streetwalkers account for most of the prostitution arrests in the United States. They are the most likely of all prostitutes to be the victims or perpetrators of crimes, and the most likely to carry venereal disease. A large percentage of streetwalkers are drug addicts.

Police records indicate that teen-agers, or "baby pros," are entering prostitution in increasing numbers. The average age of prostitutes arrested in Miami is 18, three years younger than it was three years ago. Many young girls say they are prostitutes only part-time and plan to leave the work after a few years. Included in this group is the emanicipated "swinger" who participates in sexual relations with a number of men or in a group for money.

Despite the lighthearted "for fun and profit" attitude of many of today's young prostitutes, most psychological studies show that few prostitutes are well adjusted or happy in their work, especially after the novelty wears off. Suicide and attempted suicide rates for prostitutes are far above the national average. Acute depression and insecurity, especially as the woman becomes older and less sought after, are common. Two students of the problem have noted that "It is a rare prostitute who does not feel deep down that the simplest housewife is better off than she is. But she will not admit it if she can help it."[7]

Role of Males as Homosexuals, Pimps and Gigolos

Prostitution is not exclusively a woman's calling. Male homosexual prostitution is believed to be on the increase. However, arrests are infrequent and customers are reluctant to report robberies or beatings to the police. Male prostitutes are found primarily in large cities, and they are likely to be 15 to 25 years old. The vast majority of these hustlers are bisexual although few are noticeably effeminate. The more successful among them become the "kept boys" of wealthy men— a position comparable to that of the well-established mistress.

Male homosexual brothels, known as "peg houses," are on the decline. Massage parlors, staffed by male masseurs, have to a large extent supplanted the brothels. In the March-April 1971 issue of *Trans-action* magazine, David Pitman describes

---

[7] John M. Murtagh and Sara Harris, *Cast the First Stone* (1957), p. 132.

this type of operation. The male "madam" has a staff of approximately 15 full-time "models" and 20 part-time staffers. Customers are protected against robbery and assault and their identities are kept secret. They are charged $20 an hour; the hustler receives $14 and the madam $6. Models are forbidden to engage in any sexual activity with each other and are discouraged from developing emotional ties with their clients. Brothels and massage parlors usually require periodic checks on their models for venereal disease.

The few studies that have been made indicate the clients are usually well-to-do professional men in their forties or fifties. From one-third to one-half are married. Individual homosexual prostitutes often seek clients in hotel bars and lobbies. Others use rest rooms or public baths to make contact. The least prestigious and usually the oldest and least attractive become streetwalkers. Like female streetwalkers, they make far less money and are much more likely to be arrested. Certain areas of some major cities, such as the Tenderloin district in San Francisco and West 42nd Street in New York, are known meeting places for such contacts. There is also the gigolo, who, according to tradition, is supported by rich, old and lonely women. Or he may be a free swinger, as depicted in the award-winning movie *Midnight Cowboy*, a name applied to a Times Square hustler of both men and women. His women customers were relatively young but bored wives.

While prostitution, whether male or female, has become less organized and more an individual undertaking in recent years, there is still a coterie of auxiliary personnel involved. Included are pimps, panderers, madams, doctors and lawyers, members of organized crime and, of course, the clients. The pimp is a man who obtains all or part of his income from the earnings of prostitutes. He serves them by being on the alert for the police, posting bail, getting a lawyer and handling violent customers. It is impossible to know the number of pimps operating in the country today, although it has been estimated that 90 per cent of them are black. Relatively few are arrested; even fewer are convicted. Prostitutes seldom divulge the name of their pimps to the police.

While the affection and loyalty of prostitutes for their pimps are well-established, few pimps seem to return these feelings. Most are inclined toward homosexuality; many are driven by fear and insecurity. One pimp expressed his loathing for women in general. "That's where the thrill was...in the absolute vilification, in the degradation. To be a great pimp,

I think you've really got to hate your mother."[8] Many pimps are drug addicts or alcoholics. Prostitutes who are unable to provide enough money for a pimp's expensive tastes or habits are beaten, sold to other pimps or abandoned. Prostitutes have been known to commit suicide after being left by their pimps.

The panderer or go-between serves as intermediary between prostitute and client. Sometimes the panderer might be the pimp but more likely he is a taxi driver, bartender or bellboy. Procurers are panderers who introduce a girl into prostitution. A "Murphy man" acts as a panderer, takes money from the potential customer and disappears without producing the prostitute.

Persistence of Prostitution Despite Sexual Revolution

Alfred Kinsey, in his celebrated treatise on the sexual habits of American males, estimated in 1948 that 69 per cent of them had visited a prostitute at least once.[9] Between 1940 and 1950, according to further surveys, 20 to 25 per cent of American male college students had their first sexual experience with a prostitute but by 1967 only 2 to 7 per cent did. This change was due in large measure to the sexual revolution and the widespread availability of free sex."[10]

If sex outside of marriage is so prevalent today, why is prostitution flourishing? Renni Flohr, a San Francisco psychiatric social worker, theorizes that "sex is no longer for love or procreation but solely for enjoyment." But "this leads to fleeting sexual contacts, which turn out to be meaningless. What gives them meaning is the profit."[11] For many young swingers, prostitution is no worse, less hypocritical and potentially more lucrative than most of the jobs available to them. They claim to enjoy the independence and derive satisfaction from flaunting the mores of society. As for their customers, the reasons most frequently cited by men who visit prostitutes are drunkenness, curiosity, restlessness, bravado, interests in perversions not otherwise obtainable, or simple biological necessity.

The Pill, the coed dorm and the commune, Otto Friedrich observed recently, have not done away with the streetwalker, much less the bordello. "Even in societies that have been con-

---

[8] Quoted in *Time*, Jan. 11, 1971, p. 54.

[9] Alfred C. Kinsey, *et. al., Sexual Behavior in the American Male* (1948), p. 604.

[10] See "Sexual Revolution: Myth or Reality," *E.R.R.*, 1970 Vol. I, pp. 241-258.

[11] Quoted in *Newsweek*, July 12, 1971, p. 78.

siderably more libertarian than ours, somehow the appeal of prostitution stubbornly remains," he wrote. "In emancipated Sweden, where premarital sex is considered a civil right, there are very few streetwalkers nowadays, but Stockholm still has hundreds of massage parlors, modeling studios and other such institutions.[12] The sex revolution has been good for a number of prostitution businesses. There is a well-established link between pornography and prostitution. As Gail Sheehy explained: "One promises, and the other delivers." The call girl is considered an asset to corporate entertaining.

American Prostitution and the Law

COLONIAL AMERICA had little prostitution, not because of any moral or legal sanctions but simply because there was no need for it. "Adultery and fornication were so prominent as to render the prostitute not only unwelcome but almost super- fluous."[13] The acknowledged promiscuity of men like Benja- min Franklin and Alexander Hamilton, who in spite of their illicit liaisons continued to serve their country, is some indica- tion of the tolerance in late 18th century America. But prosti- tution spread during the 19th century. Large numbers of immi- grants, many poor and unskilled, turned to prostitution as the only way of making a living. The pioneer woman was often a prostitute. On the frontier, there was an abundance of men, a scarcity of women, and the enticements of power and money.

Toward the middle of the century, the rise of Victorian morality provided an additional boost for the prostitution business. Married men who were expected to limit the grati- fication of the senses found in the prostitute an uncritical and willing outlet for their repressed drives. In 1859, Dr. William Sanger published the *History of Prostitution* in which he wrote: "The whole area of the United States is 2,936,166 square miles, and if all the prostitutes therein were divided over the surface there would be one for every forty-seven square miles, or if they were walking in a continuous line, thirty-six inches from each other, they would make a column nearly thirty-five miles long."

---

[12] Otto Friedrich, "Time Essay," *Time*, Aug. 23, 1971, p. 35.

[13] T. C. Esselstyn, "Prostitution in the United States," *Annals* (of the American Academy of Political and Social Science), March 1968, p. 126.

Throughout the 19th century, most of the laws dealing with prostitution provided punishment for the woman involved; customers and procurers were generally not pursued. In the early years of the 20th century, a number of efforts were made to deal with prostitution. In 1909, Iowa became the first state to enact a law giving any citizen or group the right to apply to a judge for an injunction to close a house of prostitution. Since that time, all other states have passed similar legislation. Citizens' committees, vice commissions and other groups joined in the battle against prostitution. Beginning in 1907, the Immigration Commission investigated the "Importation and Harboring of Women for Immoral Purposes." The commission estimated that no less than 25,000 women were recruited into prostitution each year and that at least 50,000 men and women were engaged in their recruitment.

These disclosures soon moved Congress to outlaw the transport of women from one state to another (Mann Act) and into this country (Bennet Act) for immoral purposes. There followed, by 1915, legislation enacted by 45 states prohibiting third parties from profiting financially from prostitution and providing severe penalties for those found guilty of forcing women into prostitution. Between 1910 and 1916, there were 1,537 convictions for transporting women across state boundaries for illegal purposes. Punishment was usually five years in prison and a fine of $5,000. If the girls were under 18 years old, the penalty was doubled.

Heyday of City Brothels and Red-Light Districts

The first three decades of this century saw the immense growth of the brothel, a place used exclusively for the business of prostitution. A Department of Justice study begun in 1911 estimated that there were about 100,000 women in urban brothels at that time. Vice investigations undertaken between 1910 and 1916 disclosed that there were almost 2,200 brothels in 22 American cities. Brothels were often concentrated into one area, known as a red-light district. "Tenderloins" were slightly less concentrated areas of brothel prostitution.

One of the brothel's most famous and often romanticized institutions was the madam. Usually an ex-prostitute, the madam had over-all responsibility for running the brothel. Many madams paid protection money to the police or other officials. In her autobiography, the famous New Orleans madam, Nell Kimball, wrote: "The truth is crime could not exist without some form of protection, even control from above.... Every respectable city or town has a knowing, greedy set of police officers who demand a cut.... Every house of prostitution, every criminal gang operating could be knocked out of business in a day if the proper orders were given. But police, courts, lawyers, bail bondsmen, fences, strike-breaking organizations are so bedded down with their crime contacts and in the big money that it would be against human nature to expect a fully lawful community."[14] Madams who were arrested were often charged with failure to report their income.

For the individual prostitute, brothel prostitution was the least demanding kind. She was not obliged to solicit customers or to be on the constant lookout for the police, her income was fairly regular and she had the companionship of other girls like herself. However, of every dollar the prostitute earned, 50 cents would usually go to the madam who used it to pay extortionists or officials, eight cents would go for room and board, two cents would go for medical examinations, 20 cents was claimed by pimps or other intermediaries, and the prostitute herself would keep 20 cents.[15] Prostitutes were expected to hustle liquor. Despite exorbitant prices and the fact that liquor was illegal during Prohibition, the availability of alcoholic beverages was a necessity. "Dry" brothels did little business.

By the 1920s, organized crime had taken control of prostitution in many American cities. In Chicago, Al Capone dominated the largest syndicate of brothels in the country. Buffalo, New York City, Galveston, Los Angeles and Newport, Ky., were a few of the cities where prostitution was controlled by the underworld. Gangsters forced many madams to pay protection money. A few, like John Dillinger who hid in St. Paul brothels during the 1930s, sought refuge from the police in friendly houses. Today, with the decline of the brothel and the trend toward more individualized prostitution, organized crime is probably less involved in prostitution. One authority contends that "the Mafia had, by 1970, liquidated most of their prostitution enterprises as unprofitable."[16] Others challenge this finding. The Intelligence Bureau of the Internal Revenue Service estimates that organized crime derives $225 million each year from prostitution. New York Police Commissioner Patrick V. Murphy believes that the Mafia has "considerable control of prostitution through the pimps."[17] Los

---

[14] Nell Kimball, *Her Life as an American Madam* (1970), pp. 142-3.

[15] Charles Winick and Paul M. Kinsie, *The Lively Commerce* (1971), pp. 149-150.

[16] Lester Graham, *The Sexual Revolution* (1971), p. 223.

[17] Quoted in *The New York Times*, July 11, 1971.

Angeles police say they have evidence that massage parlors serving as covers for prostitution are controlled by the underworld.

Upsurge and Control of Prostitution in Wartime

War typically increases the numbers of prostitutes and customers, as well as the efforts of governments to protect their men in uniform from venereal disease. Nell Kimball described the sexual excitement generated by World War I. "Every man and boy wanted to have one last fling before the real war got him.... It wasn't really pleasure at times but a kind of nervous breakdown that could only be treated with a girl and a set-to." The Draft Act of 1917 outlawed prostitution near military installations. Enforcement of this law and public support for it resulted in the closing of every red-light district in the country by the end of that year.

In France, an alarming rate of venereal disease among American troops prompted Gen. John J. Pershing to place all houses of prostitution off-limits. The soldiers were provided instead with "positive recreational facilities" like movies, sports and reading material. Despite all of these efforts, the U.S. Interdepartmental Social Hygiene Board reported that between September 1917 and February 1919, there were 222,000 cases of venereal disease in the army and more than 60,000 in the navy. VD was the largest single cause of loss of manpower in the armed forces during the war, and most of the venereal infections could be traced to prostitutes.

Many of the anti-prostitution measures used during World War I were invoked again during World War II. The federal government in 1940, at the start of the American military buildup, banned prostitution near military and defense centers as well as in areas frequented by military personnel. Yet many army commanders in the field felt that it was impossible to suppress prostitution. Some in North Africa, Sicily, France, Germany and the Far East tolerated prostitution under the condition that it was closely supervised. The end of hostilities in 1945 brought a great increase in prostitution in nearly all theaters of military occupation. Soldiers had considerable free time, discipline was relaxed, and prostitutes flocked to military bases.

Controlled prostitution during the Korean and Viet Nam wars has been, if not officially approved, at least officially tolerated. Korean prostitutes were readily accessible to American troops. Early in the Viet Nam war, a special brothel was built in An Khe exclusively for American soldiers. Vietnamese prostitutes there were required to have a special entertainer's card and undergo a medical examination each week. The An Khe brothel was in contrast to the many unsupervised houses in Viet Nam which contributed to a high rate of venereal disease among American soldiers. It is estimated that 200 GIs per thousand contract VD each year in Viet Nam, a rate more than six times higher than for civilians in the United States. Brig. Gen. David Thomas, senior army medical officer in Viet Nam, recommended in October 1969 that brothels be run by the military Post Exchange system. His suggestion was not acted on.

Enforcement of Vice Laws Since World War II

While prostitution was flourishing in and around military bases in the early 1940s, it was declining markedly in most American cities. Some 680 studies undertaken by the American Social Health Association in 526 communities in 1942 revealed that "in city after city law enforcement was taking hold. When the war ended in August 1945, commercialized prostitution had reached an all-time low. In many places it was almost entirely eliminated."[18]

Prostitution increased slightly in the first years after the war but far less than after World War I. A few brothels reopened and many prostitutes flocked to large city hotels and bars. Around 1950, prostitution again began to decline. Reasons frequently cited for this decline were improved law enforcement, stricter court procedures, a lessening of organized crime's control over prostitution, stronger public opinion against the prostitute and her associates, and an improved economic situation which offered women many other jobs.

Widespread toleration of prostitution which characterized the years before and after World War I was replaced by the prohibitionist view that effective law enforcement can lead to reductions in prostitution. Larger cities established vice or morals squads to cope with the problem. During the 1950s and early 1960s, there were notable reductions in the number of streetwalkers in New York City, Los Angeles, Buffalo, Philadelphia, New Orleans, Washington, D.C., Seattle, Portland, Ore., and Calumet City and Peoria, Ill.—cities formerly known as prostitution centers. Along with the decline in prostitution, there were significant drops in crime and venereal disease in these cities.

---

[18] Paul M. Kinsie, *Prostitution—Then and Now* (1953), p. 8.

The American Law Institute in 1961 included a Customer Amendment, a provision for the punishment of a prostitute's client, in its model penal code. There are now 21 states that penalize men caught patronizing a prostitute. However, many communities have been reluctant to enforce these laws, especially when they involve "respectable" citizens. Moreover, few prostitutes are willing to testify against their customers and few customers want to give evidence against a prostitute, particulary when the evidence is likely to incriminate them. Some judges have been known to let the man go if he testified against the prostitute with whom he was apprehended. Thus, while the law in many states has become stricter and more rigidly enforced, it is the woman and not her client or pimp who usually pays the price.

Anti-prostitution laws and crackdowns fall most heavily on streetwalkers. In large cities, they are likely to be poor and black. It is true that an increased concern over civil liberties in recent years has made the task of enforcing vice laws more difficult. Policemen often cannot use wiretapping to apprehend call girls. And courts have held that the policeman must wait until the prostitute approaches him and names a price before he can arrest her for prostitution. But when charges of prostitution cannot be substantiated, a woman suspect is likely to be arrested for loitering, disorderly conduct, or vagrancy.

Prostitutes who are arrested, fined, or even jailed almost inevitably return to their trade. This recidivism creates a vicious circle of arrest, court appearance, conviction and release. John M. Murtagh, a New York judge familiar with the problem of prostitution, has written: "Incarceration never 'cured' a prostitute—never did and never will. Prostitution is basically a social, medical, and moral problem. The penal approach to the problem is at best a feeble attempt to repair damage done in childhood."[19]

Controversy Over Issues of Legalization

THE MAJOR ARGUMENT for the regulation of prostitution assumes that since it cannot be eliminated, it must be controlled. With very few exceptions, American communities have rejected legalization in favor of prohibition. There were two official attempts made at regulating prostitution in the 19th

[19] Murtagh and Harris, *op. cit.*, p. 295.

century—in Nashville, Tenn., beginning in 1863, and in St. Louis in 1872. Prostitutes in both cities had to register and submit to periodic medical examinations. The Nashville experiment lasted three years. Its failure was due primarily to the reluctance of many prostitutes to register. The St. Louis regulation attempt was abandoned after one year because public opinion strongly opposed the "licensing of vice."

According to the American Social Health Association, prostitution is legal at present in the United States only in Storey County, Nev., a mining area of 700 inhabitants east of Reno. In the absence of a state law expressly forbidding or authorizing prostitution, the Storey County commissioners declared prostitution legal, effective Jan. 1, 1971, at specified locations and imposed a license fee of $1,000 a month at each location. These licenses were expected to provide the county about one-fifth of its revenues.

Prostitution has long been tolerated in Nevada. In many areas of the state it had already attained a status of twilight legality. Houses of prostitution went undisturbed if they were outside business areas or not near schools or churches. It is estimated that as of mid-1969 some 30 to 40 brothels with seven to 10 girls apiece operated in the permissive Nevada counties. Most counties required weekly medical examinations and, in many, prostitutes were not permitted to leave the brothels and mingle with other residents of the community. Brothel prostitutes were fingerprinted and given cards identifying them as prostitutes.

In California, a bill to allow prostitution on a county-option basis was introduced in the 1971 legislature but it died in committee. Assemblyman Leroy F. Greene, who introduced the measure, said that a poll in his Sacramento district showed that 69 per cent of his constituents favored legalization. Opposition to the bill came primarily from housewives, women's liberationists, police officials and clergymen.

Legalized Prostitution in Other Times and Places

Attempts to deal with prostitution have been recorded since biblical times. According to the Old Testament, the ancient Hebrews provided a market place for their harlots. Roman prostitutes were probably the first required to register. Their names were placed on an official register and could never be removed. Roman prostitutes were also taxed, required to wear distinctive clothes and deprived of many of the civil liberties afforded other Romans. Throughout the Middle

Ages, the Roman system of regulation and licensing was gradually adopted by most European cities. The outbreak of syphilis in the late 15th and early 16th centuries and the grim moralism unleashed by the Reformation led to a brief period of suppression. By the 18th century, most countries allowed prostitutes to operate provided they received periodic medical examinations. At the end of the 19th century, there was official regulation of prostitution in most major European and in some Oriental cities.

Outside the United States today, there are two major ways of dealing with prostitution—regulation and abolition. In this context, the word "abolition" refers not to the abolition of prostitution but to the abolition of laws regulating, recognizing or licensing the practice of prostitution. Abolitionism does not necessarily sanction prostitution. As explained by Abraham Flexner, "If decency is violated, if disorder is created, if neighbors are scandalized, in some countries if disease is communicated, society considers itself warranted in interfering."[20] Abolitionists generally oppose open soliciting and the right of pimps or madams to profit from prostitution. Abolition is widespread in Europe.

Regulation is employed widely in Asia and South America. Restrictions are placed on where and how a prostitute may operate. Brothels and individual prostitutes must be licensed by the police and regular medical examinations are required. In the view of one authority, regulationist countries "regard prostitution as an evil which must be endured" while abolitionist countries tend "to ignore the question of prostitution except where and so far as it can be linked with some other offense...."[21]

France outlawed houses of prostitution in 1946 but not prostitution itself. Prostitutes still had to register and, until after 1960, to have medical checkups. Italian brothels were made illegal in 1958 and free-lance prostitution, which was not banned, increased. Many European countries now follow the system in Britain where prostitution practiced by women over 21 is not illegal, but soliciting on the streets, debauchery in public places, and procuring and pimping are.

The approach to prostitution in the Soviet Union is governed in large part by the Marxist belief that it is the foremost example of the enslavement and exploitation of women.

---

[20] Abraham Flexner, *Prostitution in Europe* (1914), pp. 287-288.

[21] G. R. Scott, *Ladies of Vice* (1968), p. 138.

Prostitution in itself is not a criminal offense but the activities of pimps, brothelkeepers and other "exploiters" are. One authority asserts that in the Soviet Union prohibition is relatively successful because "the general standard of living is low, there is little leisure and the authorities are all-powerful."[22] But there is some evidence that prostitution is increasing. The Supreme Soviet of the Georgian Republic in July 1971 made existing penalties for spreading veneral disease more severe. The action was believed to be a result of prostitution activity at seashore and mountain resorts.

Nevertheless, foreign visitors report that prostitutes in most Russian cities are extremely difficult to find. One visitor wrote: "In Moscow, I failed to locate any prostitutes despite enlisting the help of newspapermen, illegal money-changers and taxi drivers. Whatever prostitution exists in Moscow and Leningrad is apparently so underground that it is impossible for the casual visitor to find."[23] Anti-prostitution campaigns have been far from successful in Eastern Europe.

Unclear Effects of Control on Disease and Crime

Prostitution is assumed to be a major source of venereal disease in America. During the last five years, the VD rate has almost doubled and for teen-agers it has increased elevenfold. The American Social Health Association estimates that in the fiscal year 1970 more than 2,375,000 cases of syphilis and gonorrhea were treated, and that statistically one American in ten is likely to get VD. Among prostitutes, some are more susceptible to venereal disease than others. Phillip Donahue, chief of Venereal Epidemiology for the Public Health Department in Washington, D.C., asserts: "As the price of a prostitute goes up—say from $20 to $50—the chances of getting syphilis goes down because the girl is dealing with a better class of clients. The high-incident VD population is the very poor."[24]

While some persons claim that close medical supervision of prostitutes can considerably reduce venereal disease, others question its effectiveness. The American Medical Association contends that "medical inspection of prostitutes is untrustworthy, inefficient, gives a false sense of security and fails to prevent the spread of infection." Likewise, the American Social Hygiene Association states: "There are no 'safe' prostitutes. No able doctor will certify a prostitute to be free of

---

[22] Lujo Basserman, *The Oldest Profession* (1967), p. 281.

[23] Harold Greenwald, *op. cit.*, p. xiii.

[24] Quoted in *The Washington Post*, May 24, 1971.

disease. But even when prostitutes are inspected by doctors, between examinations they must and do have numerous customers. Some of these customers are sure to be infected and to infect these prostitutes who pass on their disease to many others."[25]

The effects of legalization or toleration of prostitution on venereal disease have had mixed results. The closing of supervised brothels in Australia a few years ago has not significantly altered the incidence of venereal disease there. Italy's closing of its brothels was believed to be directly responsible for a sizable increase in that country's VD rate during the next few years. In Hawaii, venereal disease diminished after houses of prostitution were closed on the islands in 1944; but in Nevada, supervised houses are believed to contribute very little to the problem. Whatever their contribution to the state's venereal disease problem, many of the women in Nevada's houses of prostitution have volunteered to take part in a six-month experiment conducted by the federal Food and Drug Administration to test a drug, Progonasyl, that might prevent venereal infection.

Those favoring the legalization of prostitution believe that it would reduce the number of crimes committed by and against prostitutes. They argue that under a closely supervised system, prostitutes would be unable to rob or blackmail clients and clients would be unable to harm or abuse prostitutes. It is known that prostitutes supporting drug habits commit far more crimes than non-addicted prostitutes. It is reasoned that legalized prostitution, with its close medical supervision, would significantly reduce drug addiction.

Since the vast majority of crimes arising from prostitution are committed by streetwalkers, it is also assumed that getting women off the streets and into supervised houses would significantly reduce the crime rate. But that assumption was not borne out by the experience of Terre Haute, Ind. Its brothels were closed in 1942 and the number of robberies and assaults dropped significantly in the following year. "In terms of every important index of anti-social behavior or community problems, Terre Haute was a healthier and safer city after the brothels closed...."[26] In the case of Hawaii, police records were checked for sex crimes in the 11 months before and 11

[25] The two associations were quoted by Robert Y. Thornton in *Controlled Prostitution?* (1954), p. 5.

[26] Winick and Kinsie, *op. cit.*, p. 224-225.

months after the closing of the islands' brothels. The records indicated that fewer sex crimes were committed afterward than before. There was also a decline in juvenile delinquency after the houses closed. In describing these findings, Charles Winick and Paul M. Kinsie commented: "Although such changes cannot be directly attributed to the houses' closing, they had some relation to it."

"Even under the best of circumstances, random sexual encounters will inevitably contain elements of squalor and violence," Otto Friedrich wrote. "But it is reasonable to conclude that the sale of sex in America is not so much an immoral business as a sad and shabby one, and that legal permission plus a measure of supervision would be a genuine improvement." Likewise, the Wolfenden Report published in Britain in 1957 holds that "Prostitution is a social fact deplorable in the eyes of moralists, sociologists and, we believe, the great majority of ordinary people. But it has persisted in many civilizations through many centuries, and the failure to stamp it out by repressive legislation shows that it cannot be eradicated through the agency of criminal law."

American communities can look for advice and example to a variety of places in their dealings with prostitution—to New York City with its police crackdown, to England where there is tolerance short of disorder, or to Storey County, Nev., where prostitution is legal and licensed. Everyone knows that something must be done about the situation but no one seems to know precisely what.

COEDUCATION: NEW GROWTH

by

Helen B. Shaffer

TREND TOWARD UNIVERSAL COEDUCATION
Difficulties of Changeover in Private Colleges
Planning by Men's Colleges to Admit Women
Plans for Conversion Among Women's Colleges
Pairing of Boys' and Girls' Preparatory Schools

EVOLUTION OF COEDUCATION IN AMERICA
Origin of Coeducation in Early 'Dame' Schools
Rule of Separation by Sex in Private Academies
Public High Schools and Spread of Coeducation
Slow Growth of Coeducation Beyond High School

FACTORS AT WORK IN CURRENT TREND
Student Preference for Coeducational Colleges
Educational Benefits and Cost Considerations
Pressure to End Sex Segregation in Dormitories

1969
May 7

COEDUCATION: NEW GROWTH

O NE OF THE LAST BASTIONS of male exclusiveness—
the private men's college of liberal arts—is succumbing
to an influx of female students. Women's colleges also are
moving toward coeducation, but the trend there is less significant than the collapse of the one-sex ideal in the male
enclave. The women's colleges came into existence in the
first place largely because girls were either refused admission or given only limited and grudging access to male-
dominated facilities of higher education. In time, the wom-
en's colleges acquired a great tradition of their own to which
they clung, just as a few hundred men's colleges clung to
theirs during the years that coeducation was becoming the
norm in state universities and other institutions of higher
education.

By and large, however, the women's colleges have not
stood so firmly as the men's against coexistence of the sexes
on a single campus. Their hospitality to male faculty, for
example, has been in sharp contrast to the miniscule showing of female scholars on the faculties of men's colleges. A
male president of a woman's college is by no means unusual;
a woman president of a men's college is as unthinkable today
as it was a century ago. Similar sex differentials favor male
leadership on boards of trustees and in administrative staff
positions: the male position is strong in women's colleges
and is almost totally controlling in men's colleges.

Difficulties of Changeover in Private Colleges

A changeover to coeducation appears to present more
problems of adjustment at men's than at women's colleges.
"The whole Yale experience is geared toward men," said
Henry Chauncey Jr., special assistant to President Kingman
Brewster Jr., after the decision to admit women was made
known on Nov. 14, 1968. Apart from weightier considerations, Chauncey was concerned about an assumed demand
by women students for bathtubs in place of the shower

147

facility that is standard at Yale.[1] When Princeton on Jan. 12, 1969, announced its intention to introduce coeducation, the special trustees' committee which made the recommendation said it involved "the largest single decision that has faced Princeton in this century." The committee warned that "There are obviously risks in a new undertaking of this magnitude."

There is little evidence that women's colleges moving toward coeducation have taken so portentous a view of the change in their realm. On the other hand, the women's colleges are less likely to experience the avalanche of applications from the opposite sex that descended on leading men's colleges after they announced their fateful decision. More than 4,300 girls made formal application for admission to Yale in September 1969, when undergraduate coeducation begins at that 268-year-old institution.

Faculty and students at the colleges going over to coeducation are overwhelmingly in favor of the change, and efforts to tap alumni opinion show at least a majority willing to go along with the times. But the men's colleges are still concerned over the effect of the new policy on alumni financial support. There is some fear that alumni who are the most generous donors may include those who will be the most outraged at tampering with tradition.

Despite random expressions of doubt or dissent, the trend toward eradication of sex separation in American education appears to be irrevocable. It is occurring simultaneously with a growth of coeducation around the world in countries which had clung more tenaciously than the United States to segregation by sex in education. The United Nations reported on March 12, 1969, that among 105 countries responding to a questionnaire sent out by UNESCO (United Nations Educational, Scientific and Cultural Organization), only four—all Arab nations—still maintained complete separation of the sexes by law in education; 27 had a completely coeducational system. In Britain, Cambridge University is to admit women in 1972 or 1973 as undergraduates in a men's college (Churchill); other all-male colleges at Cambridge and Oxford are expected to follow suit.

---

[1] "Everyone knows that women prefer to take baths rather than showers, but in all of Yale College there is only *one* bathtub."—*Yale Alumni Magazine,* December 1968, p. 11.

Coeducation: New Growth

Between the 1966-67 and 1967-68 academic years, 18 all-male and 35 all-female colleges and universities in the United States took steps toward integration of the sexes at the undergraduate level. Although the total number of institutions of higher education increased by 237, the number of men's colleges declined by eight and the number of women's colleges by 35. The extent of the dominance of coeducation in higher education was indicated by the most recent U.S. Office of Education figures (1967-68) : Of a total of 2,489 institutions, only 214 were for men only and 248 for women only. The trend has been persistent in recent years. Statistical compilations for 1968-69 are certain to show even fewer one-sex colleges.

Planning by Men's Colleges to Admit Women

More significant than numbers is the standing of colleges taking the coeducational plunge. So long as institutions like Princeton, Yale and Vassar stood fast, the position of the one-sex liberal arts college seemed secure; when they fell, the cause seemed all but lost.

For a year, Yale and Vassar had considered establishing a coordinate relationship—that is, a relationship in which the two institutions would maintain separate administrations and financing but share some or all academic programs. Yale was willing, but in November 1967 Vassar turned down the plan, saying it favored coeducation but preferred to "remain mistress in our own house." The plan would have required Vassar to move from its present site in Poughkeepsie to Yale acreage in New Haven.

Yale then discarded the coordinate concept and turned to developing a plan for admitting women to its undergraduate college. The plan was approved by the Yale Corporation on Nov. 9, 1968, and by the Yale faculty five days later. It provided for admission of 500 women, one-half of them freshmen, in September 1969. The number was kept low to give Yale time and experience before settling on a final plan. By early April, college authorities had completed review of the 4,350 applications and made their selections; acceptances were sent out to 648 women—278 for admission to the freshman class and 370 for transfer from other colleges. The women in 1969-70 will represent roughly 15 per cent of the total undergraduate student body. The number to be admitted ultimately is undetermined. Cost studies were based on a potential enrollment of 1,500 women with male enrollment remaining at its present level of around 4,000.

During the same period, 223-year-old Princeton University was moving slowly in the same direction. The board of trustees in June 1967 authorized a "searching" study of the advisability of admitting undergraduate women. A year later, a faculty-administration study committee, headed by Gardner Patterson of the Princeton faculty, reported overwhelmingly in favor of coeducation. The report was immediately endorsed by President Robert F. Goheen; several months later, it was "emphatically" approved by the faculty. On Jan. 12, 1969, Goheen announced that the board of trustees had approved "in principle" the recommendation of the Special Trustees' Committee on the Education of Women at Princeton that the institution take the fateful step. The board then asked the administration to draw up a specific plan for consideration by the trustees.

Princeton announced, April 12, that it would admit 130 undergraduate women in full status in September 1969. The number would be increased in succeeding years to 375, 550, 630, and 650. The institution would embark on a construction and renovation program that would enable it ultimately to enroll at least 1.000 women without lowering the present male enrollment of 3,200.

Dartmouth College is moving cautiously toward coeducation. The Campus Conference, an administration-faculty-student-trustee body, declared in January 1969 that "the education of women at Dartmouth College is a subject of top priority." The trustees thereupon created a special committee to make an exhaustive study of the question. Meanwhile, Dartmouth is participating in a student exchange program that is breaking the sex barrier at 10 leading eastern colleges.[2] Also looking toward the future is the institution of Coed Week, initiated at Dartmouth in 1967-68 and repeated on a larger scale during the past winter; some 1,000 undergraduate women from other colleges spent the week of Jan. 22-27 attending classes and participating in other campus activities.

---

[2] The others are Connecticut, Mt. Holyoke, Smith, Vassar, and Wheaton colleges for women, and Amherst, Wesleyan, Williams and Bowdoin for men. The exchange students attend the host school for their junior year, returning to their home campus for the senior year. A special conclave of Amherst faculty, students and administration on April 24-25 approved introduction of coeducation.

Coeducation: New Growth

Men's colleges with definite plans to admit women in September 1969 include, in addition to Yale and Princeton, Franklin and Marshall College at Lancaster, Pa.; Georgetown University, Washington, D. C., which will admit 50 girls to its undergraduate School of Arts and Sciences; University of the South at Sewannee, Tenn.; and Union College in Schenectady, N. Y. Wesleyan University at Middletown, Conn., is building new dormitories to accommodate women students; it plans to admit small but increasing numbers annually until there are two women for every three men enrolled.

Colgate University in Hamilton, N. Y., expects to admit a few women in 1970. It is already housing 56 girls from Skidmore College as a coeducation tryout. A special faculty committee at Lafayette College at Easton, Pa., recently reported in favor of admitting women. Hamilton College at Clinton, N. Y., has opened a coordinate women's institution called Kirkland College. The all-male undergraduate School of Arts and Sciences of the University of Virginia at Charlottesville has been ordered to admit women by the fall of 1970; the university has maintained a separate establishment for undergraduate women, Mary Washington College, at Fredericksburg, 65 miles from the main campus. California Institute of Technology (Caltech) in Pasadena, which this year let in about a dozen women as student research associates, will open its doors to full-status, female undergraduates in September 1970. Boston College, after a year's study of the question, took action in March to admit women to its undergraduate school in 1970.[3]

Plans for Conversion Among Women's Colleges

The trend toward coeducation is even more marked among women's colleges and is encouraged by the lowering of barriers to women in the all-male institutions. Because of the reluctance of many bright girls to pursue their studies in an all-female environment, it is now taken for granted that all of the "seven sisters"[4] will become coeducational before long. "It should be obvious by now that coeducation has

---

[3] Boston College, like Georgetown University, is a Jesuit institution. Both had admitted women to their graduate and professional schools before lowering the barriers to undergraduate enrollment in liberal arts. Georgetown went still further toward coeducation: it opened enrollment in its School of Nursing to male students. The University of Notre Dame and St. Mary's College in South Bend, Ind., announced May 3 that they would take steps beginning in September 1969 to make the two schools "an increasingly coeducational character."

[4] The "seven sisters" are high-prestige women's colleges, usually designated as Barnard, Bryn Mawr, Mount Holyoke, Radcliffe, Smith, Vassar, and Wellesley.

taken a high priority at most of the eastern prestige schools traditionally segregated by sex," the editor of the Mount Holyoke student paper observed about the time Yale's doors opened to her sex.[5] Of the 370 women accepted for transfer to Yale in September 1969, 49 are currently enrolled at Wellesley and 48 at Smith.

After Vassar turned down Yale's proposal for merger, the 108-year-old women's college considered establishing a co-ordinate male college of its own but decided it would be "sounder, simpler, quicker, and cheaper" to open Vassar's doors to men.[6] The board of trustees on Oct. 19, 1968, decided to begin admitting male transfer students to Vassar in September 1969 and male freshmen students in September 1970. The present enrollment of 1,500 women will not be reduced. but provision will be made ultimately for 900 or more additional students who will be men. Some 80 male exchange students from Colgate, Trinity and Williams are already in residence on the Vassar campus.

Trustees of Radcliffe College voted Feb. 22, 1969, to open discussions with Harvard College looking toward development of the existing close relationship between the two institutions into a full merger. The Radcliffe trustees acted in the wake of considerable pressure from students of the two colleges. Sarah Lawrence at Bronxville, N. Y., founded 40 years ago to provide a distinctive and individualized program of education for women, admitted men students for the first time this year; 18 male undergraduates and six male graduate students are now enrolled along with 600 women students. Student demonstrations at Sarah Lawrence have been directed toward, among other goals, an increase in the number of male students (and more diversity in the selection of women students).[7]

Student demands for coeducation at Smith, largest of the women's colleges (2,300 students), are backed by results of a faculty poll showing that 56 per cent of the members prefer teaching coeducational classes and that only 10 per cent prefer all-female classes.[8] Faculty members expressed concern that Smith might lose many of its best students to co-

---

[5] "Coeducation Now," *Choragos*, Nov. 21, 1968, p. 4.

[6] Vassar President Alan Simpson, letter to alumnae, mailed in mid-October 1968.

[7] Sarah Lawrence had its first sit-in in March 1969 when 80 students occupied an administration building to protest a tuition increase and admission policies said to create a "rich girls' fashionable college" image.

[8] "Results of Faculty Survey on Coeducation," *The Sophian*, Feb. 27, 1969, p. 2.

educational institutions. Student pressure for coeducation is building up at Mount Holyoke, which has links of the coordinate type with all-male Amherst and the coeducational University of Massachusetts. Mount Holyoke girls now share with Amherst boys a weekly seminar in sex education. Other women's colleges moving toward coeducation include Mills College, Oakland, Calif. (500 students), Bennington in Vermont (420 students) and Connecticut College in New London (1,500 students). Connecticut College will admit its first male students next September.[9]

Pairings of Boys' and Girls' Preparatory Schools

The coeducation movement in higher education has a counterpart among high-prestige private schools. The National Association of Independent Schools has noted rising interest in coeducation among many of its member schools still segregated by sex. Though the subject was not on the formal program of the annual N.A.I.S. conference in New York, Feb. 27 - March 1, 1969, an association officer told Editorial Research Reports that there was considerable discussion of coeducation "in the halls." Interest was most marked among boarding schools at the secondary level, a group which has been most attached to the British pattern of separate boys' and girls' institutions. Only 16 of a representative N.A.I.S. group of 232 boarding schools at the secondary level are coeducational. Some of the 150 boys' schools are now seriously considering a change.

Like the men's colleges, the boys' schools face questions of how far or how fast they should go in abandoning a treasured tradition. By and large, the tendency is to choose coordination with a girls' school, if only as a cautious first step toward coeducation. Officials of a number of schools have been visiting Kent School, which recently built a coordinate girls' school three miles from its main facility for boys at Kent, Conn. An N.A.I.S. official said he knew of at least 40 schools—20 potential pairings—in its membership that were at some point along the road to uniting.

Choate School and Rosemary Hall have agreed to join as coordinates in the autumn of 1971. The plan is to move the girls' school from its present location at Greenwich, Conn., to Choate's 700-acre campus at Wallingford near New

---

[9] Still formally named Connecticut College for Women, this institution intends to legalize its recent practice of dropping the last two words in its name.

Haven; the two schools will continue to have separate administrations and faculty. St. Pauls at Concord, N. H., is
considering a closer relationship with Concord Academy for
girls. Principal Richard W. Day of Phillips Exeter Academy
in New Hampshire, like Choate a major "feeder" school to
Ivy League colleges, has formally stated his position: he
does "not favor coeducation for Exeter" but believes that "a
cooperative arrangement" with a girls' school would be "an
improvement educationally for both"; Day therefore has
urged Phillips Exeter's board of trustees to "look into the
possibility of persuading an established girls' school to move
its facilities to the Exeter area." [10]

Evolution of Coeducation in America

EDUCATION of males and females in the same class or
even within the same institution above the primary level
was a rarity until it began to take hold in the United States
about a century ago. Separating the sexes in education has
usually meant an inferior education for the female. Recent
developments in coeducation may therefore be regarded as
a late chapter in the evolution of women's rights in education. The link between "the development of coeducation"
and "increasing women's access to education" was recognized in a U.N. report showing a worldwide trend toward
"teaching boys and girls together." [11]

Coeducation was unknown to ancient Greece. In Rome,
girls joined boys in the elementary schools and women were
sometimes admitted to the advanced rhetorical schools on
equal terms with men. Among early universities, Bologna in
the 13th century admitted women. But on the whole, "from
the dawn of the Middle Ages until late in the 18th century,
social usage and ideas sharply separated the functions of the
sexes" according to a principle of male supremacy which
made little provision for coeducation.[12]

---

[10] The Phillips Exeter Academy, *The Principal's Annual Report to the Trustees,*
January 1969, p. 8.

[11] UNESCO (United Nations Educational, Scientific and Cultural Organization),
Co-Education Spreading Through the World, March 12, 1969.

[12] "Coeducation," *Encyclopedia of the Social Sciences,* Vol. 3 (1930), p. 614.

Coeducation: New Growth

Settlers in the American colonies carried with them attitudes toward the education of women that had prevailed in their home countries. By that time "the flare of interest in the intellectual improvement of the sex in Queen Elizabeth's reign had . . . died out and an era of indifference, marked, at times, by open hostility toward her education, had ensued." [13] As late as the 18th century, many of England's leading figures—Samuel Johnson, John Milton and Lord Chesterfield among them—opposed education of women beyond instruction in domestic skills. Women were believed to have neither need nor capacity for much more.

Origin of Coeducation in Early 'Dame' Schools

Among early colonists, some of the better educated families taught daughters as well as sons in the home; such families, however, were a minority. Even when both were taught at home, the education of the girl usually emphasized what was considered necessary to her future role of wife, mother, and homemaker. In time, the more prosperous families, anxious that their daughters acquire social graces, hired tutors from abroad to teach them music, dancing, fancy needlework, and French. The home-taught boys usually were subjected to a more rigorous curriculum that included Latin and mathematics.[14]

Coeducation made earliest headway at the elementary level. The first compulsory education laws, enacted in Massachusetts Bay Colony in 1642 and 1647,[15] did not specify sex of students, and localities differed on whether the requirement to set up schools for children applied to girls as well as boys. Some towns ordered schoolmasters to teach both; "generally, the number of [primary] schools receiving girls on equal terms with boys was small." [16]

Despite the limited provisions for the teaching of females, Puritan society produced some women of sufficient education to be entrusted with the instruction of very young children of both sexes.[17] Often the teacher-housewife would assemble neighborhood children in her home where she

---

[13] Stuart G. Noble, *A History of American Education* (revised ed. 1961), p. 268.

[14] August E. Meyer, *An Educational History of the American People* (1957), p. 70.

[15] The General Court (legislature) of Massachusetts required in 1647 that every town of at least 50 households provide instruction to children in reading and writing.

[16] August E. Meyer, *op. cit.*, p. 33.

[17] Only one woman in four prior to 1700 could read or write her own name. Both the increase in women's literacy and the tenor of their education in the early 18th century are indicated by the publication of such books as *The Compleat Wife or Accomplish'd Gentlewoman*, forerunners of today's women's magazines.

taught the little ones their letters. These women became known as "school dames" and later, when they had moved their activities beyond the home, their establishments became known as "dame schools." These schools grew in number and spread beyond New England; they continued to exist well into the 19th century, establishing a tradition of female teaching in coeducational primary schools which has persisted to this day.

Boys attended dame schools with girls from the ages of four to seven. They then transferred to grammar schools where they were taught by masters. Girls often remained at the dame schools beyond the age of seven to be taught sewing or other household arts. "Here and there, however, where the dame's education was adequate and the girl eager, she not only mastered the subjects taught the boys, but stayed to study arithmetic and even Latin." [18] Girls were sometimes allowed to attend the grammar schools, but only during the summer or after-hours when boys' classes were not in session, and the girls' curriculum was usually more limited than the boys'.

Rule of Separation by Sex in Private Academies

Coeducation as it prevails today is the product of a movement which started about the time of the Revolution to extend the education of women beyond the barest knowledge of the three R's, training in domestic skills and, for the richer girls, the graces of refined living. Reformers, both men and women, began to insist that it would serve the best interests of the individual, the family, the community and the nation if women received more education than had been generally available to them. Much flowery rhetoric was expended on the glories of an educated womanhood,[19] but underlying such justification was a practical need for women as qualified (and low-wage) teachers of the young in a nation that had come to recognize the value of a literate labor force.

---

[18] Mabel Newcomer, *A Century of Higher Education for American Women* (1959), p. 7.

[19] In an address published and widely circulated in 1828, a male proponent of women's education (Charles Burroughs) said: "Learning pleads for woman to bring her energies and her charms to its exalted cause. . . . It is by providing high schools of instruction for females that you are to make them the best . . . teachers in the land, to render them ministering angels to countless beings, and to multiply the joys of learning and virtue. . . ."—Thomas Woody, *A History of Women's Education in the United States* (1929, reprinted 1966), pp. 314-315.

The response to the demand for improved education for girls took the form, mainly, not of opening boys' schools to girl students, but of founding female academies or seminaries. Even the few private secondary schools that admitted both sexes made efforts to keep them apart. "The general practice everywhere was to provide separate schools or departments for girls, if any provision at all was made for them. . . . In New England, the Leicester Academy (1793) taught both boys and girls but did not admit the girls to the Latin course. Coeducation was common in the academies of Maine after 1800 and in those of Indiana after 1830." [20] Although the curricula in the girls' schools broadened along the same lines as in the boys' schools, they continued to offer "the fripperies of filigree, painting, music and drawing" and they were subject to much criticism for their trifling content.[21]

Public High Schools and Spread of Coeducation

Coeducation spread with the growth of the public high school after the Civil War. Having originated from popular pressure to extend the public elementary school upward, the high school tended to carry on the coeducational practices of the lower grades. A report of U. S. Education Commissioner John Eaton in 1883 showed how well established the custom of coeducation had become in the public schools by that time. Of 196 school systems in larger cities and towns that had answered a government questionnaire, 177 were wholly coeducational and 19 separated the sexes for at least a part of the course. In small towns and rural communities, coeducation was even more nearly universal.

The commissioner reminded the reader that "both the general instruction of girls and the common employment of women as public school teachers depend, to a very great degree on the prevalence of coeducation," and that "a general discontinuance . . . would entail either much increased expenses for additional buildings and teachers or a withdrawal of educational privileges from the future women and mothers of the nation." [22] Nevertheless, as late as 1920 there were still 78 non-coeducational public high schools in the

---

[20] Stuart G. Noble, *op. cit.*, p. 282.

[21] Thomas Woody, *op. cit.*, p. 442.

[22] U. S. Department of the Interior, Bureau of Education, *Coeducation of the Sexes in the Public Schools of the United States* (Circulars of Information Number 2, 1883, pp. 8-27.

nation, divided equally between boys' schools and girls' schools.

The New York City school system includes 18 all-boy and 11 all-girl schools, but their one-sex policy appears doomed. The Board of Education in late April agreed to admit a girl in September 1969 to all-male, science-specializing Stuyvesant High School. The girl, backed by the National Emergency Civil Liberties Committee, had filed suit with the State Supreme Court, charging discrimination on the basis of sex. The suit, still pending, is aimed at banning sex segregation in all public schools in the city.

Slow Growth of Coeducation Beyond High School

Coeducation in American higher education began in 1837 when newly established Oberlin College admitted four women students. The movement was slow to get under way. Two other colleges in Ohio had an open-door policy from their beginnings in 1844 (Hillsdale) and in 1853 (Antioch), as did the University of Deseret (later Utah), opening in 1851, and the University of Iowa, opening in 1855. But the main force of the higher-education-for-women movement before the Civil War was directed toward the establishment of women's colleges.[23] Some of these were weak extensions of colleges.

State universities were early carriers of the coeducation idea. Yet they showed some hesitancy about according women full status. The University of Michigan's original charter, issued in 1837, called for a "female department," but no money was provided for it and women did not actually enter the institution until 1870. The University of Missouri admitted women in 1870 but restricted them at first to its "normal" [teacher training] department. "Finding . . . [this] did no manner of harm," the university president reported later, "we very cautiously admitted them to some of the recitations and lectures in the university building itself, providing always they were to be marched in good order, with at least two teachers . . . as guards." [24]

By 1870, at least eight state universities were coeduca-

---

[23] Georgia Female College at Macon, chartered in 1836 and opened in 1839, is believed to have been the country's first institution of higher education for women.

[24] Mabel Newcomer, *op. cit.*, pp. 13-14.

tional; they were, in order of their acceptance of women: Iowa, Wisconsin, Kansas, Indiana, Minnesota, Missouri, Michigan and California. But the combined female enrollment at the state universities at that time was only 200. In addition, there were at least 40 private coeducational colleges with a combined female enrollment of about 600. Yet in 1870, according to statistics compiled by the U. S. Commissioner of Education, a total of around 11,000 women were enrolled in institutions of higher education. The great proportion of them were in small women's colleges or female seminaries above the secondary level; only 3,000 of the women students attended degree-granting institutions. The role of the state universities in furthering the cause of coeducation was fundamental.

> When the state universities . . . moved from the narrow class basis of the pre [Civil] war years toward the development of large popular institutions, it was to be expected that women would be included. For the state universities owed their expansion in large measure to the success with which they articulated the common schools, the high schools, and the universities. In helping the extended combined elementary-secondary schools to achieve effective high school status, the universities strengthened a public school system that had long been coeducational. As the final rung in the ladder of state-provided education, the state universities of the West were neither in a position nor in a mood to deny the fruits of higher education to its young women.[25]

The situation was different in the East where private schools and colleges had established a pattern of boys' academies funneling students into men's colleges. A major breakthrough for coeducation in the East was made when Cornell began to admit women in 1872. Although this was only three years after Cornell, chartered in 1865, had opened its doors, it was already well endowed and highly regarded as a leading representative of the "new university" idea. Meanwhile, the successful establishment in this period of women's colleges with high academic standards—Vassar, Smith and Wellesley—helped counteract popular myths concerning the evils or absurdities of higher education for women.

The proportion of colleges that were coeducational grew steadily—from 29 per cent in 1870 to 58 per cent in 1910 to more than 80 per cent today. Many economic and social factors combined to push up the percentage—the emancipation of women, the growth of occupational opportunities for

---

[25] Frederick Rudolph, *The American College and University* (1962), pp. 314-315.

them, the professionalization of traditional areas of female employment, and the growing dominance of the public institutions in higher education as a whole.

During the depression of the 1930s a number of men's and women's colleges lowered sex barriers to promote larger enrollments. During World War II certain men's colleges with flagging admissions opened their doors to women. After the war, when returning veterans with G.I. benefits competed for the limited space available in higher education, a number of women's colleges admitted men. In a number of cases policies adopted to meet emergency situations became permanent.

There remained the holdouts, still wedded to the older ideal of educating the sexes separately. The great majority of the one-sex colleges today, and those likely to be the last to change, are small church-connected institutions. There remain also the compromises with coeducation represented by the separate women's college within a larger institution —Columbia University's Barnard College, Brown's Pembroke, Rutgers' Douglass, Tufts' Jackson, Tulane's Newcomb, Case Western Reserve's Flora Stone Mather.

Factors at Work in Current Trend

CONSIDERING the dominance of coeducation in this country, the attention given to the last of the holdouts may seem misplaced. But the current interest has a valid basis. One-sex colleges introducing or contemplating the introduction of coeducation include some of the most prestigious and influential institutions of higher education in the nation. Their abandonment of a long-revered tradition marks that tradition as obsolete. It is as if vestiges of earlier concepts of the role of the educated woman in society and of the relationship between the sexes, given support by the persistence of the one-sex rule at such highly regarded institutions, were finally being swept away. "The education of undergraduate women in isolation from men," Vassar's board of trustees said, "has outlived its historical justification."

Propelling these institutions to coeducation is the concern that their high ranking in the academic marketplace may slip if they remain single-sex institutions. Men's and women's colleges are facing up to the fact that increasingly the best qualified high school graduates, like most other college-bound youths, have come to prefer a coeducational campus. That many of the present students chose the one-sex colleges in spite of, rather than because of, the one-sex rule is indicated by returns in campus polls. More than four-fifths of Princeton's undergraduates, for example, favored coeducation on that campus.

Student Preference for Coeducational Colleges

Lack of coeducation may not have been a serious handicap in the past when these institutions were unmatched in academic prestige. But the rise in stature of certain coeducational colleges and universities has weakened that competitive advantage. In addition, the great state universities now offer a distinct economic advantage because of their relatively low tuition charges.

What these factors mean to an institution that once could have the "pick of the crop" was spelled out by the Patterson report at Princeton. Princeton's appeal, the report said, was still strong; it continued to receive five applications for every available place; but it had to accept three of those five to make sure it could fill every two available spots. Furthermore, it was found on investigation, the odd man who had applied for admission to Princeton but who, on acceptance, had turned Princeton down, "often stands higher than the two who choose Princeton" by all the standard criteria—high school records, college board grades, extra-curricular activities, etc. Of 425 men identified in 1968 as "the best" among all who applied, only 181 (43 per cent) chose to enroll.

A canvass of men who had declined admission to Princeton over a two-year period showed that their principal complaints were lack of women students, inadequate social facilities, and the general social atmosphere. A former admissions officer told the Patterson committee that in visits to both public and private schools he had tried "to defend the monastic life at Princeton" but that "the old arguments simply don't sell" with "able, sensitive boys [who] take it for granted that they will sit in class with girls." The committee's own survey showed "that only 4-5 per cent of present-day students from superior secondary schools have a positive preference for an all-male or all-female college."

It was largely because of the limiting effect of its admissions policy on the pool of able young men on which Princeton could draw that the Patterson report urged the university to make the change. "Having started this study with some skepticism concerning the wisdom of Princeton's becoming significantly involved in the education of women at the undergraduate level," Prof. Patterson wrote in the report's preface, "I am now strongly convinced that this step is vital to Princeton's future." [26] Similar considerations are paramount at other high-ranking institutions. President Brewster of Yale said at the time Yale was considering an alliance with Vassar that there was "ample qualitative evidence that the absence of a first-rate women's college in the community leads many of our best potential freshmen candidates to choose to go elsewhere." [27]

With Yale and Princeton going coeducational, top women's colleges have had to face the inevitability of coeducation for them too. A Smith College faculty member said: "Smith can continue to be a first-rate school only if it decides to change. It will be a second-rate school if it decides to remain . . . [the] number one women's college in the nation." The president of Connecticut College, Charles E. Shain, said on Jan. 8, 1969, that "The number of best candidates choosing women's colleges is shrinking"; applications for admission to Connecticut College had gone down in the past two years from 1,750 to 1,425.

The problem was put bluntly by the editor of Mount Holyoke's student newspaper: "It may be extremely difficult, perhaps even sacrilegious, for some to consider giving up Mount Holyoke's claim to fame as 'the oldest continuing institution of higher learning for women in the United States,'" she wrote, "but that 'sacrifice' may be necessary if we also hope to continue to claim that we are a top-notch institution. . . . How many top students that might have come here will now prefer to choose from the new array of coed prestige schools?" [28]

Educational Benefits and Cost Considerations

The reports and statements of educators favoring coeducation reiterate now-familiar arguments on the educational

---

[26] "The Education of Women at Princeton," *Princeton Alumni Weekly*, Sept. 24, 1968, pp. 6-10, 19.

[27] *Vassar-Yale Report from the Joint Study Committee*, September 1967, p. 3.

[28] "Coeducation Now," *Choragos*, Nov. 21, 1968, p. 4.

and social advantages of this policy. They signify recognition of women's intellectual capabilities and academic attainments. They point to the daily association of men and women in business, professional and social life for which the environment of the one-sex campus is said to be poor preparation. The value of informal contacts between men and women students in coeducational institutions is contrasted with the artificiality of formal, weekend dating that characterizes the life of the one-sex campus.

Differences in the interests of men and women students, and the adjustments they would require, are recognized. Women tend to prefer courses in the humanities and social studies. In previously all-male colleges, therefore, enrollment of women would mean that a larger percentage of the total enrollment would take courses in Anthropology, English, History, Psychology, Romance Languages and Sociology and a smaller percentage would be in Architecture, Economics, Engineering, Mathematics and physical science classes. Former men's colleges would have to appoint deans of women, expand health departments, make provision not only for mixed gatherings of students but for sanctuaries where women students could get off by themselves.

Cost considerations refer primarily to the expense of providing for a larger enrollment. The small numbers to be admitted initially present a minor cost burden but ultimately an appreciable influx will call for added capital expenditures and operating costs. Yale's studies indicated that the cost of enrolling the initial contingent of women could be met by their tuition and fee charges but that to provide for an eventual total of 1,500 women would require approximately $55 million of capital expenditure.

Princeton's Patterson report indicated that admission of 1,000 women would require capital expenditures of $24.2-$25.7 million and that additional annual operating costs would exceed annual income from charges to women students by $215,000-$380,000. However, Princeton officials estimated on Apr. 20, 1969, that it would cost $8 million to provide additional facilities and $2 million of additional student aid to accommodate 650 women, the goal for 1973-1974. The university had already received a $4 million gift earmarked for coeducation, and President Goheen said "I don't believe we'll have great difficulty in raising the rest."

The trend toward ending sex segregation in prestige colleges cannot be disassociated from the pressure rising on all campuses for freer mingling of the sexes outside the classroom. Institutions going coeducational, many of which have already been pressed to liberalize or remove restrictions on visiting hours in dormitory rooms,[29] will doubtless be faced with demands for coeducational housing. Much of the student pressure for merging Harvard and Radcliffe springs from a desire for coeducational housing; Radcliffe students have been attending the same classes as Harvard men for more than 20 years.

Pressure to End Sex Segregation in Dormitories

A student-sponsored study, *Coeducation at Harvard and Radcliffe,* completed in January, urged that Harvard's house system be made coeducational. Radcliffe women complained that they could not participate in seminars and other valued activities of the houses except by invitation of a house member, and this was said to deprive them of important academic, intellectual, social and advisory benefits. They objected also to being kept "remote" from the lives of male students.

Previously all-male colleges face the problem of whether to admit women to membership in clubs. The Elizabethan Club at Yale voted May 5 on proposed constitutional amendments to remove the sex barrier to membership; an earlier straw vote indicated that 69 per cent favored the change. Similar challenges to tradition are likely to arise in prestigious societies and other organizations of once all-male campuses.

The sensitivity of women to remnants of sex discrimination in higher education is likely to assail converting colleges. Both men's and women's institutions making the changeover will try to preserve whatever advantages accrued to the separate system. Women's colleges will try to safeguard opportunities for girl students to take leadership positions in campus activities and will attempt to ensure adequate representation of women scholars on faculties. Men's colleges show little disposition to let females overrun their campuses.

---

[29] A State Supreme Court in Poughkeepsie, N. Y., rejected on April 18, 1969, a petition for an injunction, brought by the mother of a Vassar student, against recent relaxation of rules at the college. The rules now permit men to visit women in their dorms at any time. See "Sex on Campus," *E.R.R.*, 1963 Vol. II, pp. 943-962.

CHILD ADOPTION

by

Mary Costello

IMPACT OF SOCIAL CHANGE ON ADOPTIONS
Birth Control and New View of Unwed Mothers
Fewer Adoptable Infants; Black Market Demand
Rise of and Opposition to Interracial Adoptions
Attempt to Place Older and Handicapped Children

SOCIETAL VIEWS AND U.S. ADOPTION LAWS
Early View of Orphans as Objects for Indenture
Beginning of State Legal Protection After 1850
Growing Emphasis on Well-Being of the Adopted
Placement of Foreign Children in American Homes

MOVES TO OVERCOME ADOPTION BARRIERS
Use of Adoption Exchanges and TV Advertising
Procedures for Termination of Parental Rights
Trend Toward Subsidizing the Cost of Adoptions
Psychological Adjustment of Adopted Children

1 9 7 3
June 27

CHILD ADOPTION

A DECADE AGO couples unable to have their own children could expect, provided they met certain requirements, to adopt healthy infants who might even resemble them physically and mentally. In the last few years, however, the number of adoptable infants has shrunk and the couples, if they are choosy, have found the search difficult and often fruitless. Healthy white and even black babies now have no trouble finding adoptive homes. One reason for the turnabout is the increased availability of contraceptive devices to unmarried women, particularly young girls who in the past provided a large proportion of the illegitimate, adoptable infants.[1] Another factor is the relative ease in obtaining legal and illegal abortions. More important, many single women who have not taken advantage of birth-control or abortion services are choosing to keep their babies, often with the encouragement of social workers and agencies. The stigma attached to unwed motherhood is rapidly disappearing in an age in which premarital chastity has become the exception rather than the rule.

Ursula M. Gallagher, a specialist on adoptions at the U.S. Office of Child Development, told the National Conference on Social Welfare in Chicago on May 29, 1972: "At the same time that fewer white infants—and, recently, fewer black infants—are available for adoption, the number of potential adopters continues to rise. In the past, the majority of couples considering adoption were childless and turned to adoption only after they found it impossible to have their own children. Today, many couples are considering adoption for different reasons. Some believe they have a responsibility to provide a home for a child who needs one. Some who have several children feel competent to share their love with yet 'one more'; still others who *could* have more biological children prefer to adopt a child rather than add to the total population. Many single persons, too, believe they can offer love and security to a child."

---

[1] Through the years, close to 90 per cent of the children offered for adoption were born out of wedlock.

Still another reason for the increase in adopters is the relaxation of social-agency requirements. Age, income, housing, neighborhood, marital status, fertility, employment of the potential mother and even race and religion are often looked at as less important than interest in and desire to care for a child. In fact, adoption agencies typically tell would-be parents who are willing to accept only a healthy infant that they can expect to wait several years without any guarantee that the baby they want will ever be available.

The National Center for Social Statistics—an agency of the U.S. Department of Health, Education, and Welfare's Social and Rehabilitation Service—has recorded the following number of children adopted nationwide through 1970, the latest year for which official statistics have been compiled:

Year	Number	Year	Number
1960	107,000	1968	166,000
1965	142,000	1970	175,000

Since that time, several cities have indicated that the upward curve had crested locally. Fewer children were being adopted—presumably because there were fewer children available to adopt. The Los Angeles County Adoption Department reported that between mid-1971 and mid-1972, some 1,217 had been placed for adoption in contrast to 2,503 in 1967-68. The department director, Walter Heath, noted that "The waiting time for an Anglo [white] baby by an approved family is presently two years or longer, compared to an average of six to eight months five years ago."[2]

Fewer Adoptable Infants; Black Market Demand

Many persons wanting a child but unwilling to wait several years turn to the black or gray adoption market. In the black market, legal procedures are bypassed, birth certificates are falsified and available children are sold to parents unwilling to apply through the normal channels. Gray market or "independent" adoptions involve the placement of a child by anyone but a licensed agency. The usual go-betweens are lawyers, doctors, nurses, relatives, friends and clergymen. Persons wishing to adopt a baby through the gray market usually pay the mother's medical expenses and sometimes an intermediary's fee.

A lawyer described as a go-between in a number of "independent" adoptions told the St. Louis *Post-Dispatch* that "when the hospital bill alone could be $1,000, the average

---

[2] Quoted by Ray Zeman in the *Los Angeles Times,* Nov. 21, 1972.

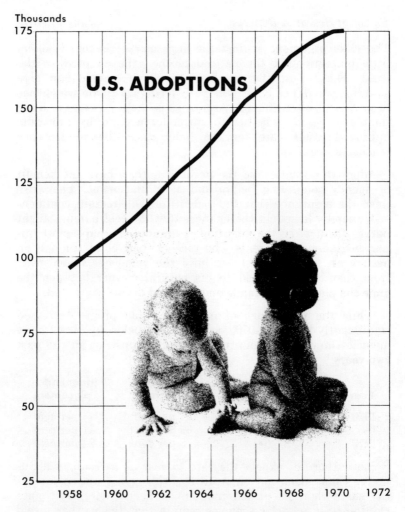

Thousands

U.S. ADOPTIONS

175

150

125

100

75

50

25

1958 1960 1962 1964 1966 1968 1970 1972

cost to the adoptive parents would be $3,500; $4,000 at the outside." He justified his $2,500 fee by insisting that if he charged by the hour for the time and effort his services required, "the cost would be astronomical." Another lawyer indicated to the newspaper that the price of obtaining a baby on the black market was indeed astronomical. "In the New York-New Jersey area, healthy white infants go for between $15,000 and $25,000," he said.[3]

While procuring an adoption for profit on the black market is illegal in all states, gray-market operations are proscribed only in Delaware and Connecticut. In these two states, licensed social agencies are required by law to arrange all placements.

---

[3] Both quoted by Jean Ehmsen in the St. Louis *Post-Dispatch*, Oct. 2-3, 1972.

The chief argument against the gray market is that it offers little protection for the natural mother, the adopters or the child. For the mother, a licensed social agency can give assurance that her child will be placed in a home which has been carefully scrutinized. Agencies also help mothers who are unable to decide whether to surrender a child by providing approved foster care for the baby until the mother has reached a decision.

Adoptive parents, like the natural mother, have the benefit of agency counseling before and after placement. They also have the assurance that their identities will remain confidential, thereby lessening the chances that the real parents might harass them after the adoption is granted. Perhaps most important, adoptive parents who receive their child through an agency are far less likely to have the youngster taken away from them and returned to his natural mother between the time the placement is made and the final decree is granted.

While the percentage of independent adoptions decreased significantly through 1970, as estimated below by HEW, many agencies around the country reported an upswing in the past two years:

Year	Children adopted by non-relatives	Agency placement	Independent placement
1960	57,800	57 per cent	43 per cent
1965	76,700	69 per cent	31 per cent
1970	89,200	78 per cent	22 per cent

Some authorities expect the rate to soar as a result of a Supreme Court decision[4] on April 3, 1972, giving unwed fathers the same right as unwed mothers to keep their illegitimate children. Since social agencies require that the mother reveal the name of the child's father, it is thought that many mothers will release their children through private channels rather than risk the possibility of a contested relinquishment. The late Pearl S. Buck, the author who worked extensively for and with homeless children, suggested nine years ago: "Since there are not enough agencies to render adoption services either to available children or to couples seeking children to adopt, the reasonable course would be to recognize the inevitable existence of the gray market and supply legal fortification for it, with protection for child and parents."[5]

Another aspect of the adoption picture is an increased willingness of Americans to adopt children of another race.

---

[4] Stanley *v.* Illinois.
[5] Pearl S. Buck, *Children for Adoption* (1964), p. 198.

Interracial adoption on an organized basis can be traced to the 1950s.[6] But it was not until the late 1960s that significant numbers of white parents began to seek out black children. A national survey conducted by Opportunity, a division of the Boys and Girls Aid Society of Oregon, found that 7,420 black children were adopted in 1971. Of these, 2,574 were placed with white families (35 per cent). There were 2,274 such adoptions in 1970 (35 per cent), 1,447 in 1969 (33 per cent) and 733 in 1968 (28 per cent).

Rise of and Opposition to Interracial Adoptions

Two principal reasons for the increase in interracial adoptions are ascribed to a dearth of white children and a liberalization of American racial attitudes. A report by the Child Welfare League in May 1970 showed that in the previous year there were 116 prospective homes for every 100 white children awaiting adoption but only 39 for every 100 non-white children available. But in December 1972, *Tuesday Magazine,* a black supplement published in many newspapers, could report: "For the first time in eight years...the number of Black normal infants available for adoption is less than the number of adoptive parents wanting them. Across the country, these infants up to the age of about two or three are finding homes as fast as agencies can handle the interviews and paperwork." The vast majority of black children in need of adoption are two or older.

A growing black consciousness, combined with a shortage of black babies for adoption, has spurred opposition to interracial adoptions. The National Association of Black Social Workers said at its 1972 convention that "the practice of placing black children in white families" was "a growing threat to the preservation of the black family" and should be halted by all public and private agencies. Some of the participants insisted that if black adopters could not be found, it would be better for the children to remain in foster homes or institutions rather than to be placed with white families.

Black families, faced with what they considered disinterest or hostility on the part of social agencies and the courts, have in the past tended to avoid the adoption bureaucracy by taking in the children of relatives and friends. A study by the Children's Bureau and George Washington University,[7] found:

[6] More than 2,000 Korean orphans were brought into the United States and an American Indian adoption project was undertaken jointly by the Bureau of Indian Affairs and the Child Welfare League. See David Fanshel, *Far From the Reservation* (1972), pp. iii-ix.

[7] *Families for Black Children: The Search for Adoptive Parents* (1971). A second publication, *Families for Black Children: The Search for Adoptive Parents, II, Programs and Projects,* was issued in 1972.

"There are more unofficial adoptions in the black community than official adoptions through agencies." It is only in the last few years that many of these agencies have tried to recruit black social workers and direct their efforts toward the black community. The first specifically black social agency, Homes for Black Children, was set up in Detroit in May 1969.

Attempt to Place Older and Handicapped Children

With a scarcity of available infants, black or white, social workers and agencies have been giving more attention to placing older and handicapped children. The Peirce-Warwick Adoption Service of the Washington Home for Foundlings, the oldest private adoption agency in the District of Columbia, decided early in 1973 to work "almost exclusively" on finding homes for the approximately 2,500 hard-to-place older and handicapped children in the area. For potential parents unable to pay the agency fees, which range up to $1,250, services will be offered free. "Peirce-Warwick's change in policy represents a direction likely to be taken by other adoption agencies as they have fewer infants available for adoption."[8]

Alfred Kadushin, professor of social work at the University of Wisconsin, has written: "The older child is, supposedly, a damaged child. He is different from the infant available for adoption in that he is more likely to have experienced deprivation and discontinuity of mothering, the trauma of separation, and a sense of rejection and loss. The older the child, the older the emotional problems...and the more resistive such problems are to change. Such considerations make adoptive applicants hesitant to accept an older child." Nevertheless, Kadushin concludes that "older children can be placed for adoption with expectation that the placement will work out to the satisfaction of the adoptive parents. The level of expectation of satisfying outcome is only slightly lower than that which might be anticipated in adoptive placement of infants."[9]

Despite the need of these children for adoptive homes, many are relegated to foster homes or institutions because their natural parents refuse to legally surrender them. The courts have been reluctant to release these children for adoption through a declaration of permanent neglect or abandonment. In recent years, however, some social agencies have assumed an activist role in working to free them either through parental consent or judicial action.

---

[8] Betty Medsger in *The Washington Post*, Jan. 20, 1973.
[9] Alfred Kadushin, *Adopting Older Children* (1970), pp. 3-4, 211.

There is some evidence that many a young unmarried mother who chooses to keep her infant later regrets the decision and surrenders the child after a few years. "Increasing numbers of unwed white mothers are having their babies and keeping them. Just how long they'll keep them, though, remains to be seen.... In San Francisco, sometimes a bellwether for youth trends, mothers 12 to 15 years old are starting to bring their babies in for adoption once they find out they can't live within welfare allowances."[10]

Some unwilling to relinquish their children permanently are turning to foster care. The California Social Welfare Board reported recently that foster-care placements in the state had doubled since 1964. "Translating this statistical data," the board said, "provides just one more piece of evidence of the inescapable result of a growing social disorganization, family disruption and a breaking down of individual and family responsibility."[11]

More difficult to place than older children are those with physical or mental handicaps. The Child Welfare League *Standards* stated that "Adoption should not be considered for children whose physical or mental condition is such that they require permanent care in a facility other than a family home." Agencies have become more flexible about allowing handicapped children to be placed for adoption; only those with the most serious and untreatable problems are now excluded.[12]

Societal Views and U.S. Adoption Laws

ONLY IN THE PAST 100 years has the well-being of infants and children been given much consideration in adoptions. While many children may have benefited as a result of formal and informal adoption in other eras, the emphasis was on serving the would-be parent. Kadushin writes: "For the ancient Greeks and Romans, adoptions were arranged to acquire an heir, to perpetuate the family name and to give continuity to a family line. In India, adoptions could provide a male child in order to meet the demands of religious ceremonials....

---

[10] Joseph Morgenstern, "The New Face of Adoption," *Newsweek*, Sept. 13, 1971, p. 67.

[11] Quoted by Lynn Lilliston in the *Los Angeles Times*, April 1, 1973.

[12] "The Adoption of Mentally Retarded Children," *Children*, January-February 1968.

Adoption among primitive groups was often for the purpose of making a captive, or a member of an 'out group,' a member of the 'in group' of the tribe, thus enhancing the economic and military power of the captors."

Children with serious physical or mental handicaps were commonly tortured, ridiculed or placed in solitary confinement. The custom in ancient Greece and Rome was to kill them. For the Romans, the first to formalize adoption in the courts, the child had to resemble, as closely as possible, a biological child and the adopters had to be 15 years older than the child and unrelated by blood. Until 291 A.D., females could not adopt nor could a female child be adopted. The Romans provided that the child be completely assimilated into the family and given all the rights of the natural child, including inheritance.

As the collapse of the Roman empire gave way to the feudal period, the feudal lord took responsibility for all the persons in his charge. "Thus the children may have been ill-treated or neglected, but they were never outcasts," Felix Infausto has written. "Adoption as we know it, reappered in Europe under the Code of Napoleon. This Civil Code of 1804, which was based on Roman law, recognized adoption, but only persons over twenty-one could be adopted and only those over fifty could adopt. The Code Napoleon and the adoption laws of all European countries...were primarily concerned, not with the interests of the adoptee, but with inheritance rights."[13]

Early View of Orphans as Objects for Indenturing

In early America, children without homes were placed in almshouses, poorhouses or taken in by relatives. Placements were usually informal and without any legal safeguards for the child. Under such a system, the adoptive parents could keep or dispose of the youngster in any way they wished and the natural parents could, if they had the will or the money, reclaim their offspring. A practice called indenturing was also common. The usual method of indenture was to apply to the poorhouse, sign a contract agreeing to house and feed the child and to teach him a skill. When the indentured child was old enough to earn his living, the money he made for several years would go to the person holding the contract.

If the children sent to poorhouses or orphanages in the 19th century were not taken in by townspeople as they grew older, they were sometimes sent to the western frontier where farmers

---

[13] Felix Infausto, "Perspective on Adoption," *Annals of the American Academy of Political and Social Science,* May 1969, pp. 3-4.

and settlers needed their labor. As described years afterward: "Trainloads of children from large eastern orphanages would tour through the Midwest stopping at every large town. The children would line up on the high depot platform forming a single line according to height, and local citizens would simply point out the girl or boy they wanted. The unchosen children would then climb back on the train and travel on to the next stop." If the child was unable to handle the task for which he had been chosen, he was often abandoned.[14]

Beginning of State Legal Protection After 1850

By the mid-19th century, the plight of homeless or indentured children was beginning to receive attention. There were no adoption statutes in any state until Massachusetts passed the first "social conscience" law in 1851. Other states followed, but slowly. A report accompanying a bill for a New York adoption law in 1865 said: "The total absence of any provision for the adoption of children is one of the most remarkable defects of our law. Thousands of children are actually, although not legally, adopted every year; yet there is no method by which the adopting parents can secure the children to themselves except by a fictitious apprenticeship, a form which, when applied to children in the cradle, becomes absurd and repulsive."[15]

New York did not succeed in making adoption subject to judicial supervision until 1873. By that time, 12 states had protective statutes. They were Massachusetts (1851), Pennsylvania (1855), Indiana (1855), Georgia (1855-56), Wisconsin (1858), Ohio (1859), Michigan (1861), Kansas (1868), California (1870), Maine (1871), Rhode Island (1872), and North Carolina (1872-73). Some other states required record-keeping of private adoptions but imposed little or no supervision over the placement and welfare of the child.

About the time that states began enacting laws to provide at least a modicum of protection for adopted children, social and philanthropic agencies were trying to improve conditions for those in custodial care. Charles Loring Brace, the Protestant minister who founded the New York Children's Aid Society in 1853, pushed for a more personal and less institutionalized type of care than the kind provided in orphanages and almshouses. Brace and his co-workers are usually credited with

---

[14] "What to Do About Adoption? A Doctor, Lawyer, & Social Worker View Their Roles," *Journal of the Mississippi State Medical Association,* January 1961.
[15] Quoted by Helen L. Witmer, et al., "The Purpose of American Adoption Laws," *Independent Adoptions: A Follow Up Study* (1963), p. 20.

initiating foster care in the United States. Children were placed in the homes of families who offered to care for them for a fee without actually adopting them.

To some, foster care was not a panacea but a potentially more damaging experience for children than institutional care. Orphanages, for all their defects, offered the child some continuity of care and many psychologists reasoned that repeated changes in foster homes could be unsettling and hurtful.[16] Anna Freud and Dorothy T. Burlington responded in their 1944 study, *Infants Without Families,* by saying: "When choosing between the two evils of broken and interrupted attachments and an existence of emotional barrenness, the latter is the more harmful solution because it offers less prospect for normal character development."

Permanent placement in a loving home, according to virtually all authorities, offered the child the best chance for normal character development. During the late 19th and early 20th centuries, in an effort to protect youngsters, several states tightened the regulations governing adoption. Michigan passed a law in 1891 to require a judicial investigation of the potential adoptive home and family. In 1917, Minnesota became the first state to require all private and public adoption agencies to make a thorough investigation of adoptive homes, to protect adoption records and proceedings and to provide a supervised trial period before the final adoption decree could be approved.

Growing Emphasis on Well-Being of the Adopted

The Child Welfare League *Standards* stipulates that: "The placement of children for adoption should have as its main objective the well-being of children.... The main purpose of an adoption service should not be to find children for families, nor should it be expected to provide help for many of the problems associated with childlessness." During the first three decades of the 20th century, considerable progress was made in changing the emphasis from the parent to the child. Social work was recognized as a profession and social agencies, staffed by professionally trained men and women, developed standards and guidelines for adoption. The U.S. Children's Bureau, the Child Welfare League of America[17] and numerous

---

[16] In contrast, Dr. Margaret A. Riddle, in her book, *The Rights of Infants* (1943), pointed out that foster care had virtually eliminated marasmus, a progressive emaciation of youngsters, which, at the turn of the century, was responsible for more than half the deaths of institutionalized infants.

[17] CWLA, founded in 1920 and headquartered in New York, describes itself as "the only privately supported organization devoting its efforts completely to the improvement of care and services for the nation's deprived, neglected and dependent children."

state and local agencies for children in need of adoption were established at this time.

Despite these advantages, many potential adoptive parents were discouraged from applying to an agency because of rigid socio-economic and religious requirements, long waiting periods and overly personal and embarrassing investigations, including fertility examinations, conducted by inflexible and often tactless social workers. While these practices were instituted to protect the child, they frequently drove those who wanted a youngster to the gray or black market.

By the early 1950s, as the number of non-agency placements skyrocketed, child welfare authorities began reassessing and changing their adoption standards. A British observer noted in 1968: "The effect of America's radical reappraisal is that their assessments of applicants and children are more flexible and the child's urgent need now dictates American adoption policy. Couples are no longer turned down almost automatically because of middle age, a divorce, no formal religion or a low income. Nor are they refused because they have their own children."[18]

Religion, however, can still be a troublesome issue in adoption proceedings, according to Sylvia Gollub, a social worker. Writing in the magazine *Church and State*[19] in March 1973, she said 35 states required that, "when possible" or in similar prefacing words, the judge give custody only to persons of the same religious faith as the child. "Curiously," she wrote, "this is the only parental right of many recognized by our society (including determination of the child's living standards, education, earnings, inheritance) which is singled out for such protection in an adoption."

Placement of Foreign Children in American Homes

Faced with the shortage of adoptable American babies, many would-be parents have turned in recent years to homeless foreign tots. The Immigration and Naturalization Service reported that between mid-1971 and mid-1972, 3,023 children from other countries were brought into the United States for placement in American homes. Of these, 957 had been adopted by Americans in the children's own countries and 2,066 were admitted under a pre-arranged plan for formal adoption in this country. The largest number—1,585—came from Korea; 355 were from Canada; 204 from Germany and 119 from South Vietnam.

---

[18] Diana Dewar, *Orphans of the Living* (1968), pp. 148-149.

[19] Published by Americans United for Separation of Church and State.

ADMISSION OF IMMIGRANT ORPHANS FOR ADOPTION

Region of birth	1948-57 Average Number	Per Cent	1962-68 Average Number	Per Cent	1972 Number	Per Cent
Europe	561	73	676	41	361	12
Asia	206	27	916	56	2,114	70
North America	—	—	27	2	444	15
South America	—	—	3	—	63	2
Africa	2	—	8	—	23	1
Australia/New Zealand	1	—	11	1	12	—
All other	2	—	4	—	6	—
All countries	772		1,645		3,023	

SOURCE: Adapted from U.S. Immigration and Naturalization Service data

Foreign adoptions have been arranged privately on a small scale since the 19th century, but it was not until after World War II and particularly the Korean War that large numbers of foreign children were taken in by American families. Concern for the children orphaned or displaced by war is generally cited as the major reason for these later adoptions. A number of agencies, including the International Social Services (ISS) and the organizations established by Harry Holt, the Oregon farmer, and Pearl S. Buck,[20] aided in finding homes for war-ravaged, unwanted or destitute foreign and mixed-blood children.

In the 1950s, many foreign and mixed-blood children came to the United States through a procedure known as proxy adoption—defined by the CWLA *Standards* as the "legal adoption of a child in one country by parents residing in another who are represented in court abroad by proxy." The 1953 Refugee Relief Act approved the proxy adoption-visa arrangement and Congress in 1957 extended it for three more years over the opposition of social agencies."

Despite this condemnation, Mrs. Buck defended Holt's use of proxies for Asian children. "The proxy method was the only one approved by the Korean government, which at that time was anxious to get the half-American children out of Korea as quickly as possible. Any other method was interminably slow

---

[20] ISS, founded in 1921 and headquartered in New York, acts as a go-between for American social agencies and those in foreign countries in finding homes for children. Harry Holt, the founder of the Holt Adoption Program Inc. at Eugene, Ore., used proxy adoptions, among other methods, to bring Asian children to the United States. Pearl S. Buck set up Welcome House in 1949 to find permanent American homes and families for children of mixed American-Asian parents and the Pearl S. Buck Foundation to care for those born of American fathers and Asian mothers who could not leave the country where they were born.

and the children often grew too old or died in orphanages before they could get to their American families."

The war in Vietnam has brought thousands of requests from American families for Vietnamese children orphaned by the fighting or fathered by U.S. servicemen. However, the Saigon government has been reluctant to release full- or part-Vietnamese children for adoption in the United States. According to the Immigration and Naturalization Service, only 362 Vietnamese children were admitted to the United States between 1964 and 1970. Later figures are not available. Nor is it known how many Vietnamese children are in need of homes; estimates on the number fathered by American GIs range from 5,000 to more than 20,000.

While the children of Korean mothers and American fathers are unacceptable to ethnocentric Koreans, the treatment of mixed-blood children in Vietnam often depends on the father's race. "The Vietnamese take fairly good care of Caucasian-Vietnamese offspring. The children of black GIs and yellow Vietnamese mothers, however, suffer the most. They are given away, according to Sister Sabina of Go Vap, because 'people here in Vietnam are ashamed of the Negro children and in some orphanages keep them apart from the other children.' "[21]

In the past 25 years, the number of foreign adoptions by Americans has increased fourfold *(See opposite page)*. Intercountry, like interracial, adoption has become an area of growing controversy. "The proponents say the primary reason for such adoptions is direct humanitarian service to needy children and to prospective parents. The opponents argue that no child should be transplanted from his own culture, nationality and race and asked to bear the burdens of possible rejection and loss of identity."[22]

Moves to Overcome Adoption Barriers

THE SEARCH for adoptable youngsters has been hindered by the lack of a nationwide centralized reporting system. Pearl S. Buck spoke nine years ago of the need for unified adoption processing which "will make it possible for adoption agencies to search the nation for the right child for the right home." In

---

[21] Quoted in "Walter Scott's Personality Parade," *Parade,* Feb. 4, 1973, p. 2.
[22] John E. Adams and Hyung Bok Kim, "A Fresh Look at Intercountry Adoptions," *Children,* November-December 1971, p. 214.

recent years, a number of organizations have been formed to find homes for children across geographical boundaries. The most publicized of these is the Adoption Resources Exchange of North America (ARENA), established in 1967 by the Child Welfare League. ARENA functions as an information exchange in the United States and Canada. Agencies supply the organization with the names of children and agency-approved adults wishing to adopt, and it disseminates the information to the participating agencies.

Many state and private agencies have also set up networks for placing children. The oldest state adoption information bureau—the Illinois Department of Children and Family Service's Adoption Information Service—was begun in 1963. This tax-supported exchange works with agencies throughout the state to find homes for adoptable children. And on the private level, Charles Filson, a Presbyterian minister in Illinois, established a non-profit multiple-listing service known as Child Care Association in September 1971. The organization sends a booklet to subscribers with a picture and information on the age, race, personality and medical history of adoptable children. Within a year after it was established, CCA had about 90 subscribing state, county, and church-affiliated adoption agencies in the United States and Canada and had placed more than 200 children.

Another way of finding homes for children and youngsters for parents desiring them is through the mass media—television, radio, newspapers and magazines. The oldest of the televised adoption programs is "The Ben Hunter Show," which began in October 1967 and is broadcast for 15 minutes each week on station KTTV in Los Angeles. The Los Angeles County Department of Adoptions works closely with the show. Children available for adoption are shown with their caseworkers or sometimes with their foster parents. "There is general agreement among [the department's] staff that when infants and young children are 'made visible', they sell themselves."[23]

Procedures for Termination of Parental Rights

The Children's Bureau has estimated that about 60,000 children in the United States are in need of adoption. Other organizations calculate that the number could be as high as 100,000. However, the majority of these children are not legally free for adoption; their natural parents refuse either to care for them or to surrender them for others to adopt. Joseph

---

[23] Children's Bureau, *Families for Black Children* (1972), pp. 10-11.

STATE ADOPTION LAWS

State	Permits independent placement	Permits independent adoption	Offers subsidy	Requires judicial termination of parental rights	Requires father's permission in case of unwed mother
Ala.	Yes	Yes	Decided in each case	Yes	
Alaska	Yes	Yes	No	Yes	No
Ariz.	Yes	Yes	For medical care	No. Voluntary consent accepted	In some cases
Ark.	Disapproves but not prohibited		In some cases	Yes	Yes
Conn.	No	No	For medical care	Yes	If he acknowl- edges paternity
Del.	No	No	For medical, boarding	Yes, in non-relative adoption	No
Fla.	Yes	Yes	No	Yes	No
Ga.	Law prohibits	Yes	No	No	In some cases
Hawaii	Yes	Yes	In some cases	Yes	No
Idaho	Yes	Yes	No	Yes, when term in- voluntary	In some cases
Ill.	By parent, guardian, or court		Medical in some cases	Yes	Yes
Ind.	By mother or judge		No	No	In some cases
Kan.	Yes	Yes	Medical, aid to parents	No	No
Ky.	With approval of Commissioner of Child Welfare		Boarding, in special cases	No	No
La.	Yes	Yes	No	No	If he acknowledges paternity
Maine	No	Yes	No	No	No, but under study
Md.	By mother or her parent(s)		Medical care under Title XIX funds	Yes	Subject to court's decision
Mass.	By mother only		Yes	No	No
Mich.	Yes	No	Yes	Yes	Yes
Minn.	In specific cases	Yes	For wards of state	Yes	Yes, as policy, pending new law
Miss.	Yes	Yes	Not specified	No, accepts voluntary consent	No

181

State	Permits independent placement	Permits independent adoption	Offers subsidy	Requires judicial termination of parental rights	Requires father's permission in case of unwed mother
Mo.	Some courts permit		No	Yes	No
Mont.	Yes	Yes	For handi-capped children	Yes	No
Neb.	By mother	By mother or court	For medical, legal	No	No
Nev.	In some cases	No	Yes	No	No
N.H.	Yes	No	In some cases	No	No
N.J.	With mother's consent	No, court appoints agency	Legislation pending	In non-relative cases	In some cases
N.Y.	Yes	Yes	Medical	No	No
N.C.	Yes, but not encouraged	No	No, with rare exceptions	No	No
N.D.	By mother	By step-parent relative	Yes	No	No
Ohio	Yes, by probate court	No	Yes	No	In some cases
Okla.	Yes	Yes	During trial period for adoption	Yes	If he acknowledges paternity
Ore.	Yes	State studies all such cases	Yes	No	No
S.C.	Yes	Yes	Not specified	Agency requires, law doesn't	No
Texas	Yes	Yes	No	No	No
Utah	Yes	Through lawyer	No	No	Yes, if known
Vt.	Yes	When relatives adopt	For foster parents who are adopting	Yes	No, but under study
Va.	No	By relatives, step-parents	Legislation pending	No	Yes
W.Va.	Yes	Yes	No	No	No
Wis.	If parents or court approve	No, agency assigned by court	No	Yes	No, but change pending
Wyo.	Yes	Yes	No	No	No

Source: U.S. Office of Child Development survey in January 1973. The following states and the District of Columbia did not reply: California, Colorado, Iowa, New Mexico, Pennsylvania, Rhode Island, South Dakota, Tennessee, and Washington.

Morgenstern has noted a trend on the part of some adoption agencies "to conduct constant, case-by-case inventories to find out why children are in long-term foster care and, when possible, to spring them from their legal limbo. This means helping the natural parent make a clear-cut decision to keep or not keep a child. Failing that, it means urging the court to make one. It means an activist role which some basically conservative agencies resist."[24]

Even the courts, traditionally opposed to severing the natural parent-child relationship, seem more inclined to free the youngsters. In October 1972, a decision by the Iowa Supreme Court indicated that the children of retarded parents could be placed for adoption. The case involved twin daughters taken away from their parents several years earlier on the ground that the infants did not receive proper care.

To date about 20 states have some provision for the involuntary judicial termination of parental rights. The others, according to the Office of Child Development, "have surrender, relinquishment, or release provisions, which are contractual arrangements with a social agency. The Children's Bureau considers these contractual arrangements unsatisfactory because the rights and obligations of the parents and children remain unclear, the child's status is uncertain and there are questions as to whether the natural parents' rights have actually been terminated."[25]

In states that do not require a judicial termination of parental rights before the child is placed in an adoptive home, the natural mother or father generally has from six months to a year between the time the placement is made and the final adoption decree is granted to reclaim the youngster. Adoption agencies typically make every effort to ensure that the natural parents will not change their minds, and they rarely do. If their initial decision leaves any room for doubt, social workers often recommend that the child be placed temporarily in a foster home until the natural parents have time to rethink their decision.

Trend Toward Subsidizing the Cost of Adoptions

In the past, only a middle- or upper-class family was likely to adopt a child who was not a relative. For the poor—both black and white—the cost of acquiring and raising a youngster plus the traditional agency insistence on economic self-sufficiency had the effect of excluding potential but less-

[24] *Newsweek,* Sept. 13, 1971.
[25] Stated in the Office of Child Development pamphlet "Termination of Parental Rights and Responsibilities and Adoption of Children," issued August 1971.

affluent adopters. In the last few years, some subsidies have become available to lower-income familes who want but cannot afford to care for children. In September 1965, New York became the first state to offer adoption subsidies to parents needing them. Since that time, many other states have enacted similar legislation. The average state subsidy grant is under $800 a year. In contrast to this relatively small expenditure, each adoption is estimated to save the state at least $40,000—the amount needed to care for a child in a public, tax-supported institution. The subsidies available for adoption are considerably less than those for care in a foster home. Nevertheless, the records show that many foster parents are choosing to adopt the youngsters placed with them, despite the lowered subsidies.

Adoption agencies also have provided subsidies to parents, particularly those who are willing to accept handicapped children. Employers offer a third, and as yet largely untouched, source of financial assistance. International Business Machines (IBM) Corporation pays up to $800 in adoption fees incurred by any of its 148,000 employees. R.C. Johnson & Sons, the wax-making company at Racine, Wis., offers a $500 adoption benefit. Both plans are relatively new; Johnson's was begun in 1970 and IBM's in December 1972.

In the last 50 years, public prejudice against the adopted child as the inheritor of an unmarried or neglectful woman's undesirable traits has largely given way to concern about the psychological adjustment of the child. The generally accepted view is that a child should be told about his adoption at a relatively young age. However, Dr. Joseph G. Ansfield, a psychiatrist, wrote in his book *The Adopted Child* (1971): "Everybody doesn't have good luck with this early, frank, honest approach, and...parents should...feel free to do whatever is most comfortable for them..."

Another accepted norm of adoption practice—the notion that it is better for an adopted child not to seek out his natural parents—is likewise being questioned in some quarters. In these and other areas of adoptive policy, hard and fast rules must often give way to the perceived needs and well-being of the individual child. The demise of the baby glut and the increase in the number of potential adopters may mean that children will be more assured of a good and loving home. It may also mean that many Americans wanting a youngster will be left with the choice of giving a foster home to an older or handicapped child for a few years or surrendering the joys of even short-term parenthood.